STORIES FROM THE

Heartland to the Pacific

STORIES FROM THE
Heartland to the Pacific

JUDY A. VASOS

Pen Stroke Press
Oakland, CA

Stories from the Heartland to the Pacific
By Judy A. Vasos

Published by
Pen Stroke Press
3048 Madeline Street
Oakland, CA 94602
www.judyvasos.com
judyvasos5@gmail.com

Text copyright © 2025 by Judy A. Vasos

All rights reserved. No part of this book may be reproduced, transmitted, or stored in an information retrieval system in any form or by any means, graphic, electronic, or mechanical, including photocopying, taping, and recording, without prior permission in writing from the publisher.

ISBN: 978-0-9997425-0-1 (print)
ISBN: 978-0-9997425-1-8 (e-book)

Library of Congress Control Number: Pending

Publisher's Cataloging-in-Publication
(Provided by Cassidy Cataloguing Services, Inc.)

Names: Vasos, Judy A., author.
Title: Stories from the Heartland to the Pacific / Judy A. Vasos.
Description: Oakland, CA : Pen Stroke Press, [2026]
Identifiers: ISBN: 9780999742501 (print) | 9780999742518 (ebook)
Subjects: LCSH: Vasos, Judy A. | Cancer--Patients--Biography. | Women--United States--Biography. | Families--Middle West. | Iowa--Biography. | Oakland (Calif.)--Biography. | LCGFT: Creative nonfiction. | Autobiographies. | BISAC: BIOGRAPHY & AUTOBIOGRAPHY / Memoirs.
Classification: LCC: RC265.6.V37 A3 2026 | DDC: 362.1969940092--dc23

Editor: Gail M. Kearns
Copy editor: Cindy Conger
Book and Cover Design: Peri Gabriel Design
Book production coordinated by To Press & Beyond,
www.topressandbeyond.com

Printed in USA

Contents

Preface — 1

Love and Pain — 5

My Grandmother — 11

Our Favorite Childhood Game — 13

Keene Funeral Home — 15

Betrayal — 19

First Heartbreak — 23

The Right Person — 25

My Short Modeling Career — 29

North Beach — 33

King's Dream, My Nightmare — 35

What I Know About the Ocean — 39

The Kidnapping of Jeff — 41

Providential — 45

Instinct — 49

Heating Up — 51

The End of It — 57

The Scar — 59

Easy Transition — 63

The Nunnery — 67

Aunt Edith — 71

Car Magic — 75

Separation — 79

Magic in the World — 81

Perfect Timing — 85

Our Luck with Mom — 87

Spin Cycle — 89

My See-Saw Mind — 93

Sister Loss — 99

The High Cost of Loving — 101

Jason's Story — 105

Remembering Carla — 109

A Day in Eschau — 113

Natalie and Kokoschka — 119

Unclaimed — 127

Acknowledgments — 131

About the Author — 133

To Jason

Front row left to right: Don Vasos, Mickey Hausman, Judy Vasos, Donna Hausman, David Hausman.

Back row left to right: Grandma (Anna) Hausman, Pat Vasos, Grandpa (Chris) Hausman.

Photo taken in 1944.

Preface

THIS IS A COLLECTION OF STORIES written between 1999 and 2024 that span my younger years living in Iowa and my life today in Oakland, California. My grandparents and many aunts, uncles, and cousins were a mainstay in my early life. When I consider the strongest influence, it's my Grandpa Hausman, my mother's father, whose kindness and love shaped me the most.

My mother, brother, sister, and I spent lots of time on my grandparents' farm ten miles from where we lived in Carroll, Iowa. My dad was in the Navy and my mother suffered from depression. The relatives on the farm helped us to manage.

We traveled the ten miles in the caboose of the Chicago Great Western train that left the busy depot in our small town of Carroll and went through Halbur, where my grandparents lived. In the winter months, we stayed warm in the caboose from the heat of the wood-burning stove fed by the conductor, a man who was always friendly to Mom and us three kids during the trip. We were the only ones who traveled this route in the caboose, and with each trip he warmed us not only with the wood stove fire but also with the attention he gave us.

The train stopped at the bottom of the hill close to my grandparents' farm. Our family trudged up the hill into the welcoming arms of my grandparents. Their smiles and hugs made us all happy, especially since Mom's nagging depression had created an almost permanent sad and sour look on her face. Our grandparents looked into our eyes and exploded with happiness to see us. We knew we were in good hands.

When I was older, I accompanied Grandma to her huge, bountiful garden across the gravel driveway and through a gate, to gather the colorful peas, carrots, tomatoes, salad greens, and whatever else she needed to prepare dinner for Grandpa and the rest of us. We'd stop on the way back to the house to pick fruit for dessert and a flower to decorate the kitchen table. It was all so natural and, in retrospect, idyllic.

As I got even older, Grandpa let me go out in the field to bring in the cows for milking. I felt so adult and capable, well aware of his complete confidence in my ability to take on this responsibility. Skippy, the dog my Uncle Nick had left on the farm when he enlisted in the Army, went with me, just as he always did with Grandpa.

Skippy was my steady companion. He knew exactly where the cows would be and remained calm while he helped lead them back through the gate. I opened and closed the gate carefully, aware of the size and power of the cows and my own power to complete this task that Grandpa had assigned to me.

When Grandpa ate lunch in the field with the other farm workers, Grandma packed his lunch—usually a sandwich of meat and cheese on her homemade bread—with a thermos of hot coffee and fresh milk added. She pointed me in the direction Grandpa was working and handed me the lunch to take to him. I loved this job and, as usual, took it seriously. I sat down on the ground with Grandpa and his fellow workers, and gave him his lunch as he introduced me to the other men. He always poured me some of the hot coffee and milk from the thermos. The mixture of coffee and milk was just right, and I never had this anywhere else until I was grown. I assumed coffee was off limits for me then, and appreciated Grandpa breaking the rules.

It was also Grandpa who showed me how to dim the lights of the car at night and turn them back on bright after passing another vehicle. He sat in the front seat with me while I was driving his car and patiently instructed me in the timing of the dimming and then the exact moment to turn them back on. It was like being let in on a secret of the universe, one that made me feel I was moving into adulthood.

He didn't holler or scold me as my father did when I was learning how to drive a car. Dad had no patience with me, but Grandpa's patience was boundless and put me at ease.

My mother once said after observing Grandpa and me together, "That's not my dad. The way he acts around you and your siblings is foreign to me." Apparently, Grandpa was not always so patient and kind with his own children.

One story that illustrates my connection with Grandpa involves a time when I was lost and didn't know the direction my life should take. I'd received a master's in social work and worked for many different agencies as a social worker. I worked mostly with young kids. I loved the kids and the idea that I could make a difference in their lives, but I knew nothing then about setting limits and boundaries, so all my energy went into the children. I realized I had nothing left for my own life. I was running on empty and knew next to nothing about who I was. I left social work, and, at the same time, I left the man I'd been living with for ten years. Both seemed too toxic to maintain.

I needed a new start. I was living in a beautiful house in the desirable Noe Valley area of San Francisco. I'd dabbled in writing, painting, and other creative activities, but had no trust that they heralded a new pathway for me. I felt at a loss and confused.

One early morning, I felt the presence of Grandpa in my room. He had died several years before, but he had a message for me: I was on the right track and should keep moving toward the creative goals that were nudging me. He said that he could see further into the future and that everything would work out okay if I would trust the creative urges.

I wasn't aware of having called on Grandpa. It was as if he appeared unbidden with this most needed message. I trusted my grandfather and saw him as a good, kind man. All of my earlier experiences with him informed me that he was reliable and spoke the truth. He was offering me confidence on a very different path that was unfolding. I had expected social work to be my career forever. I didn't understand the concepts of change or new possibilities. But here was Grandpa, long dead, coming back to encourage me to open to the new life he saw for me.

He was the perfect messenger—a grounded Midwest farmer, a holy man who had sung beautifully in St. Augustine's choir since he was a young man. A family man who had raised nine children on the farm and was now once again helping his granddaughter, who was in need of guidance. Though I'd have to go through many challenging experiences that would help change my outlook on life, he was right about the direction it was moving toward: a more creative life with a focus on writing.

Grandpa died at St. Anthony Hospital in Carroll on June 23, 1974. A nurse found him dead on the floor after he had fallen out of bed. It was probably a heart attack. There was a huge funeral at his former parish church, St. Augustine's Catholic Church in Halbur, which I did not attend. At the time, I didn't know the power of funerals. I underestimated how much it would mean to see people gathered to demonstrate their love for Grandpa and to hear my Uncle Bob and Aunt Kate singing "Panis Angelicus" and other songs he had once sung in the choir. I regret not being there. It was my own level of unconsciousness that kept me from going. I'd like to think Grandpa understood.

Love and Pain

RENOWNED CHINESE-BORN WRITER YIYAN LI WROTE, "Wondering about a person whether real or fictional, often moves the start of a story." The quote hit me after I had written a story about my great-nephew, Tommy, who lost both of his grandmothers two years apart. Tommy's grandmothers played an enormous role in his development. I felt deep empathy for him. How, at the age of six, could he understand the loss of two such important people in his life? When I finished the story, I realized something was missing: hidden within the folds of Tommy's story was my own story of the temporary loss of my parents before I was three.

The first loss came in the middle of World War II. Despite the fact that my father was married and had two children under the age of five, a category that would have exempted him in the early years of the war, he received a draft notice. In November 1943, a month shy of my second birthday, he left to serve in the United States Navy.

He wasn't sent overseas and never fought in any battles. He held a clerical job in Norfolk, Virginia. We were too young to appreciate that he was in no danger of being killed in a battle; we only knew he was away from us for two years.

His absence was devastating. The first word I'd uttered as a baby was "Dada." The question I asked my mother every day after he left was, "Is Daddy coming home today, Momma?" He sent a photo of himself in his Navy uniform, handsome and smiling. My mother told me later I talked to the photo and kissed "daddy goodnight every night."

I clung to my mother, my grandparents, and my aunts and uncles to ease the pain of missing Dad. I discovered as an adult that Mom was writing Dad daily letters with descriptions of my latest words and antics. In one letter, she wrote, "Bill, you should see little Judy, the way she crawls up the steps just like a little monkey." In another, "She's always on the go," and in another, she remarked how much I loved playing with Uncle Bobby and how Grandpa loved it when I crawled up and sat in his lap.

There was a sweetness to Mom's letters, and in reading them, I could tell she was paying close attention to my development and sharing it in great detail with Dad. Dad wrote back with equal sweetness and love, calling me his little "Blondie," and putting lots of x's as kisses for Mom, my older brother, Donnie, and me. Dad asked Donnie to take good care of Mom and me while he was away.

Given the circumstances (Mom left with two children to raise without her husband), things were going along well enough with the help of Grandma and her family. In July 1944, nine months after Dad left, another child was born: a girl they named Patricia, Pat for short. The addition of another child to care for was too much for Mom, and she went into a severe depression, later diagnosed as postpartum depression. Pat was a fussy baby, and according to an entry in my grandmother's five-year diary, "could not keep her milk down."

Written at the same time are Grandma's entries about Mom's deepening depression. Grandma writes, "Irene stayed in bed again today," and in another, "We took Irene for a ride today to cheer her up." Then, on September 11, 1944, the entry reads, "We drove Irene to Omaha today and admitted her to

St. Mary's Hospital for her depression." The love and concern for Mom were evident in all of Grandma's writing.

As an adult going through an emotionally disturbing time, I found out more by calling my parents. My friend, Jerry, a practicing psychotherapist, suggested talking to them to learn if there had been any trauma in my early life. When I asked them what might have happened to me, they seemed ready for my question. Mom said, "Do you want to tell her, Bill?"

Dad told me the details as if he'd been rehearsing and waiting for this day. He told me Mom had a nervous breakdown when I was little, and she was hospitalized. I asked, "What happened to us kids?" The same calm, steady recitation of facts. "You went with my sister, Aunt Edith, from Boone. Don stayed with Grandpa Vasos, and Pat was with Grandma Hausman." I could feel my heart ripping open at the thought of being separated first from Dad, then Mom, and finally my brother and sister.

Those separations had lodged in my body as stress and free-floating anxiety for years, long before I knew the facts to make any sense of the pain I was feeling.

Before I could fully absorb what Dad was telling me, it would take years of counseling; searching through the diaries and letters written during this chaotic time; reading books on healing, taking workshops and classes on healing, and a long stint learning about the pain of my inner child and how to reach her after all those years to help heal her wounds.

Years later, I learned that Mom received shock and insulin treatments at the hospital in Omaha: both wiped away parts of her memory. I also learned that one day in the hospital, she remembered that she had children. Thus began her discharge after a month in the hospital. Dad was still in the Navy when Mom picked us up from our respective caregivers. At Aunt Edith's, she reached out to hold me, and I was too afraid and untrusting to go to her. I ran to Aunt Edith instead and clung to her apron. Mom wrote Dad, "Can you imagine, Bill, my own daughter did not want to come to me?" During the visit, I was talking, but Mom couldn't understand what I was saying. Aunt Edith knew and interpreted my words. This was another blow for Mom, but understandable for a developing little girl who hadn't seen her mother for a month, an eternity in my mind. I'd learned to trust Aunt Edith, who had lavished me with love and attention. Aunt Edith and I were both inconsolable when Mom left with me.

We gathered up Donnie and Pat and made another go at being a family. Dad would be in the Navy for another year, so there were more letters, photos, and gifts. These were the treasures I would study as an adult, looking for signs of love and care from both my parents. It was there, but it would take me a long time to uncover it. In one photo taken when Dad was reunited with us, I have a sour look on my face—a sign it would take many years to heal the pain of separation, the broken places in our family.

Eventually, we stabilized as a family again, and life got better. I smile when thinking about the performances Pat and I put on in the living room for our parents. They sat on the sofa while we sang songs for them. One song that brought clapping and tears was "My Daddy Is Only a Picture." My sister and I put a lot of practice into this one. We belted out the words, "My Daddy is only a picture in a frame that hangs on the wall," as we swept our hands up to a framed picture of Dad hanging on the living room wall. We had no idea we were singing about children who had lost their daddies to the war. Our dad was there on the sofa, clapping, and we were beside ourselves with our entertainment skills. It was my mother and her flow of tears that made the connection between this song and the photo of Dad in his Navy uniform, the same photo I spoke to and kissed goodnight when he was separated from us. She probably relived that time of brokenness each time we sang the song. I didn't have a clue then why she was crying, only appreciation that our singing moved her.

Now, I view the performances as entry points to the love and care my parents felt toward us, which paved a road to healing after the painful rupture. How else could I have let love in from so many people as I grew up if there had not been an entry point created in those early years? How else could I have married a man who still explodes with love and care after forty years of marriage? How could I have welcomed a dog into my life who taught me loyalty and tenderness and heartbreak when she died? How could I be lucky enough to have found friends who were pillars of support during my two bouts with cancer? How could I appreciate all these gifts and more if I had not received love and become familiar with the shape of it?

That's why I was moved to write this story: not merely to recount a painful part of my life, but to feel gratitude for the love that was there within the chaos and pain, even if I didn't recognize it at the time.

There was enough love for me to make it in the world, to carry me to adulthood, to love and be loved, and to live fully with all my pain *and* my joy.

And that love made all the difference.

My Grandmother

Why do I wish to remember my grandmother?
Maybe because she saved me from being mute.
How did she do that?
She looked into my eyes and opened her ears
to everything I had to say.
I learned how to live by her steady gaze.
Her attention.

Now I know this was a gift.
A gift I can give to others by
looking intently and listening when
their life force is wanting to be expressed.

I can do this—give them my attention
and keep my grandmother alive at
the same time.

Our Favorite Childhood Game

AS A KID, WHEN IT SNOWED in Iowa (and it snowed a lot in Iowa), I couldn't wait to bundle up and go outside with my younger sister, Pat, or Patsy as we called her then, to create snow angels. All we did was lie down in the virgin white snow that covered our front yard and swiftly move our arms and legs up and down at the same time. Voila! We had made snow angels.

Next, we carefully and slowly lifted our bodies up without disturbing the designs we had created in the snow. Once we were standing, we looked back at our magnificent snow angels—something that didn't exist until we created them. That act of creation contained so much happiness, and we marveled at our achievements.

"Look at this one," I'd shout out to Patsy. "Beautiful, Judes. Look at mine." We both agreed we were great artists who had done something completely marvelous just by lying in the snow and moving our arms wildly.

Snow has fallen several times in California, where I now live. I suppose I could drive up to the nearby Sierra Madre mountains for snow or fly to Colorado to make snow angels. Still, I long for the freedom and comfort of stepping out the front door of our home in Iowa with my sister after a snowstorm, throwing ourselves on the snowy ground, and flapping our arms and legs magically to create the most beautiful snow angels together.

Keene Funeral Home

MY FRIEND BARB AND HER PARENTS lived on the second floor of their three-story white house, which looked like a mansion to me. Their home was, to say the least, unusual. I mean, who has caskets in their basement? But, as kids, when Barb and I got involved in playing games, we tended to forget we were in a funeral home, a forbidden and irresistible place to play. The lush, padded coverings inside the caskets looked comfortable and inviting. I often fantasized about crawling into one and taking a short nap just for fun, but I never did out of fear that Barb might close the lid. Anyway, activities in the casket room were definitely off limits.

One day, Barb and I were chasing each other really hard, running fast on the porch. I remember feeling hot and sweaty and completely exhausted when I collapsed against the front door with enough force that it opened with a bang. Unfortunately, Mr. Keene, Barb's dad, was inside at his big desk with a woman sitting in a chair in front of him. They were making funeral plans for her recently deceased husband. I got a quick glimpse of the woman as she pressed a white cotton handkerchief to her eyes, dabbing the tears that were falling. I knew right then and there I was in trouble.

I heard the scrape of his chair as Mr. Keene got up abruptly, a mean scowl on his face, and came toward me, twirling his arms to increase his speed. I felt trapped, like a helpless animal.

We moved out of earshot of the woman as he told me in no uncertain terms to stay away from the porch and not to play in this area. He made a fist and pounded it hard on the railing to emphasize his anger. Barb was nowhere in sight. She'd completely vanished, leaving me alone to deal with her dad.

Mr. Keene had no mercy. He told me I owed him a formal apology for this terrible infraction and instructed me to call him and set up a time to make my amends. I was of two minds about this request. Part of me felt grown-up enough to schedule a meeting with him. Another part of me was humiliated because I'd have to tell my parents about the incident and actually have to place the call. At that time, I only called my grade school friends. I had no reason to call adults except my grandparents to ask when they were coming to visit.

I met Mr. Keene at the appointed hour and sat in the too-large-for-me chair the woman who'd been making funeral arrangements had sat in. I had practiced the apology with my parents, but as I looked at Mr. Keene across from me, none of what I'd practiced seemed right. I relied on a basic line stolen from the *Mister Ed* television series and said in the most adult and serious way, "I'm awfully sorry, Mr. Keene."

And that was it, kind of like going to confession, but at a big table where we could see one another instead of the dark wooden confessional box that separated you from the priest to whom you confessed your sins and asked for forgiveness. Good thing I'd had that experience, or I might not have been able to pull off this formal apology.

Shortly after this incident, Barb had a Saturday night party. I heard about it, but was not invited. I was hurt, confused, and desperate, so I swallowed my pride and called Barb a few days before the party and asked what she was doing on Saturday.

"Oh nothing," she said, and then I knew that the penance for falling against the funeral home door and disturbing her dad was exclusion from Barb's party. I was sure everyone at the party would know what I'd done, although I never mentioned or talked about it with anyone.

Many years later, I saw Barb at a high school reunion in Las Vegas, an obnoxious event filled with gossip and cigarettes. She was dressed elegantly, and I recalled the time in high school when she pulled open a drawer in her bedroom and showed me all her many gorgeous pajama sets, all neatly folded. I was envious of her cool PJs.

Several times at the reunion, when Barb was not around us, she became the butt of jokes and unflattering stories, as was done with many classmates in high school. It was a cliquish thing that I had always found awful.

I did not join my former classmates in their cutting words about Barb. In retrospect, I must have forgiven her for disappearing when her dad chastised me. In Las Vegas, I found Barb interesting and her conversation stimulating compared to the banter I was having with the rest of the group.

Nevertheless, I remember feeling a mix of embarrassment and a sense of initiation into the adult world after the incident at the Keene Funeral Home in the small town where I grew up. It still stings that I was not invited to Barb's party because of my faux pas with her dad. Yet, I felt proud that I hadn't sought revenge at the reunion by participating in the rumors about Barb, and was glad that I'd gained some wisdom in the intervening years.

Betrayal

MY GRADE SCHOOL FRIENDS AND I roller-skated every Saturday afternoon. My very best friend, Lavonne, was always there.

One Saturday, my friends and I were lost in the music as we skated around and around, over and over again, in the circular rink with its colorful lights, which contributed to our altered state of mind. I felt full of energy.

Out of the blue, the music was turned off, and we all stopped skating to listen to the announcement of a special skate routine that involved breaking into two separate lines. Each of us could choose the line we wanted to join. There was no doubt about the line I wanted to be in: the one my best friend Lavonne was part of. I followed her confidently to the line she'd chosen, sure she wanted me there as much as I wanted to be there. It just felt natural.

I locked my hand in Lavonne's. Directly across, our friend Maxine stood in the other line. Maxine waved her hands and motioned for me to join her and the other friends in her line. I was flattered she liked me enough to want me in that line, but I knew I would stay true and remain with Lavonne. I shook my head no.

Maxine then motioned for Lavonne to come to her line, and to my great surprise, Lavonne immediately dropped my hand and quickly skated over to join Maxine. Everything went into slow motion as I focused on Lavonne joining hands with Maxine. *How could she be doing this?* My constant stare did nothing to bring her back; instead, she and Maxine broke into talk and laughter and didn't even look my way.

I had been betrayed at the roller rink by my best friend! Betrayal had been the last thing on my mind. Actually, it was a word I'd never thought of or used before.

It took all the energy I had left in my body to lift my heavy hand and risk reaching for the hand of the new person next to me. The broken line was reconnected, but inside, my heart was broken, and I was filled with fear of being alone and unwanted. I'd been so light and buoyant when we had begun skating, but now I moved as if there were concrete blocks rather than skates on my feet.

I faked being cheerful the rest of the afternoon so no one would know how down and damaged I felt. All I could think about and see in my mind was Lavonne skating away from me without a word. I wished the special skate routine had never been announced, wished that we could all have kept skating around together innocently and forever.

When the music stopped for the day and the skate ended, Lavonne came up to me real friendly-like to say goodbye. She said she'd call me that night to check on what I was going to wear to the basketball game the next day. I tried hard to act like nothing had happened, that everything was normal.

We talked that night and went to the basketball game the next day, but I began looking at Lavonne differently. Something inside me had changed. I may not have had the word for betrayal, but knew I had tasted the shock of it.

In adulthood, I learned that betrayal is a normal emotion that most people feel at some point in their lives; an emotion you don't usually die from, though it feels like you might when it's happening. You skate through it, taking betrayal and a long list of other unpleasant experiences with you. These experiences become a part of you, shaping who you become.

I never spoke with Lavonne about this incident, but it has stayed with me all these years. Betrayals never really leave us. Maybe we just learn to live with them. Or maybe betrayal is an opportunity to reluctantly learn something you don't want to know and accept about the universal human experience.

First Heartbreak

I SAW THE NAME LOREN SANDERS, class of 1959 in the Kuemper High newsletter, listing all the alums who had given money for the annual phonathon, which raised funds for the school's general expenses. Loren, someone I hadn't thought about in years but at one time thought I couldn't live without, came instantly alive.

We were making out in his car in front of 517 West 7th Street, my family home in Carroll. I was lost in Loren's embrace when I noticed the front porch light going on and off. And it wasn't an electrical problem. I knew it was Mom sending me a signal that I was out too late and should come in. I couldn't pull myself away from Loren's warm embrace, so I tried to ignore the flashing light. But then I saw Mom's face pressed up against the car window. She was frantically gesturing for us to roll it down. She looked desperate. We complied.

"Judith Ann," she said, using my full name to indicate the seriousness of the moment. "Do you know what time it is? You need to come in right this minute!"

I reluctantly released myself from Loren's arms and gave him a quick goodbye kiss. I was so embarrassed that I practically crawled out of the car as I followed Mom into the house. "You're grounded for two weeks," were her last words to me before I sulked off to my room.

I don't know if this incident caused Loren to break up with me, but he announced it shortly after. I cried inconsolably for days, and guessed it was the end of my romantic life. Who could ever replace Loren?

One morning, I was sitting at the kitchen table having cereal for breakfast. Mom was keeping me company and trying to offer support for my broken heart. I said, "Mom, I'm so sad and don't think I'll ever get over losing Loren."

She gently placed her hand on my back as tears began falling. I was lost in a great waterfall of tears when Mom said, "Your tears are falling into your cereal bowl." We both smiled, then laughed, and for several precious moments after, I was able to turn off the spigot of my tears and appreciate Mom's gesture of comfort.

Above his name in the Kuemper newsletter was the name Janet Kanne Sanders. I figured that must be his wife. Is that who he left me for all those years ago? If so, I hoped she is as happy in his embrace now as I was when Mom broke the spell and ordered me into the house. Thankfully, I was wrong about never getting over Loren.

Now, I'm married, and he's married, but not to each other. As fate would have it, everything works out in the end.

The Right Person

I WAS HOME ON SPRING BREAK during my sophomore year at St. Mary College in Leavenworth, Kansas. My mother was recovering from a nervous breakdown she'd had shortly after I left for college the year before. Her doctors gave her electroshock treatments again.

My studies in psychology and sociology had given me a glimpse of the suffering she was enduring. I was due to return to college and eager to see improvement in Mom's condition before I left. She was on antidepressants, but, unfortunately, she seemed to be worse.

One afternoon, she called out for me with more desperation in her voice than I'd heard before. I went into her bedroom, and she grabbed my arm to make sure she had my attention.

"Judy, I'm scared of being alone," she said. "I don't think I can make it without you here."

She didn't mention suicide but clearly conveyed her despair by the look in her eyes and her increasingly tight grip on my arm.

I felt a deep divide open up inside me as I watched and listened to her. I loved her and wanted her to get well, but I questioned whether I could give up my dream of completing college and having a life of my own.

I needed help. Why I called the local church is somewhat of a mystery. I'd begun questioning the church's teachings, but, as a baptized Catholic, priestly advice is all I knew. I'd attended Catholic grade and high schools in Carroll, and later, a Catholic girls' college.

When I told the woman who answered the phone at the church rectory of my need to talk with someone, she set up an appointment with Father Francisco that afternoon. Father Francisco was a newly arrived priest at St. Lawrence parish in Carroll. I'd never met him, and he turned out to be warm and welcoming, young, and handsome.

In grade school, I'd been exposed to the rote learning of the Baltimore Catechism (the standard book in grade school and the bible for religious training) by an older priest, Father Pecos, who snored and fell asleep in the middle of instructions. I stared at him during his naps and studied the thin red lines in his face, as well as his nose hairs, and I came close to fainting because of his bad breath. He expected my classmates and me to pay attention to questions in the Catechism: "Who made you?" This was always followed by the answer, "God made you." "Why did God make you?" "To know, love, and serve him." Page after page of profound questions followed by the most simplistic answers. No wonder he fell asleep, and I lost interest.

By contrast, Father Francisco was so full of energy that he practically bounced into the room. He looked me in the eyes, smiled, and touched my hand. He was alive and receptive, and I couldn't take my eyes off the dark black hair and his dark eyes. I figured he was Italian, though he spoke perfect English.

I instantly felt comfortable with him, and it was easy to tell him about the problem that was tearing me apart. I felt I needed to choose between the health and life of my mother and returning to college.

"Is it selfish to think of my own needs?" I asked him. "What if my mother kills herself after I leave? How would I deal with that?"

Father Francisco listened carefully and responded with the exact words I needed to hear. "This is your life and college is important to you," he said. "You can't give that up for your mother. Even if she kills herself, you have to do what is in your heart to do."

I couldn't believe it. How had I come to the exact right person? How had this stranger known precisely what to say?

I returned to college, graduated, and then went on to graduate school in social work. Mom got better. Father Francisco moved to another parish. I never saw him again. Without his wise counsel, I could have devoted my entire life to Mom and her well-being. By releasing me from the oppression of guilt, he put me in touch with my own deep need for learning and the stimulation of college.

Sometimes the right person comes along at the right time, often when you least expect it. He taught me an invaluable lesson that has served me well: to listen to the wise counsel of my heart, even when it conflicts with the needs of other very important people in my life.

My Short Modeling Career

THE AD JUMPED OUT AT ME. It described a unique chance to train as a model. I don't remember the exact wording, but it went something like this: "Fast, Easy, Don't hesitate, Call today!" I cringe when I think about it now.

I called immediately and arranged an appointment for the next day. I lived in Kansas City and had been scouring the job ads for weeks, convinced I would find an extraordinary opportunity. Was this it?

I wasn't exactly into clothes, so it took me a while to find the right outfit. This was the sixties, and Twiggy was all the rage. Finally, I donned a flattering, semi-professional look: a blue skirt, white blouse, and black jacket. I gazed at myself in the full-length mirror and wondered if I really was modeling material. After envisioning myself being photographed with elephants, laden with jewels on my arms, fingers, and around my neck, I decided I was. I imagined traveling far and wide to exotic locations. I was mapping out this perfect job and craved this exciting future.

With a feeling of magic and destiny, I arrived at the modeling agency and gave the friendly but hard-to-read receptionist my perfect smile, hoping she would notice what a good model I'd be. The part of me that had wondered what on God's good earth I was doing in this modeling agency after my years as a social worker was now totally gone.

The receptionist introduced me to the man who would conduct the interview. He stretched out his hand to shake mine, then swooped me into his office with his arm in mine as if we were in a parade being watched by thousands of onlookers.

He talked enthusiastically about the many opportunities available to me in the modeling world. Coupled with my fantasies, I was swept away, but not enough to ignore the high cost of the program. Before I had a chance to tell him I couldn't afford the program, his phone rang. He kept a steady eye on me as he responded to the caller. "Yes, yes, I know what you mean. I'll tell her."

Beaming with happiness, like we'd just gotten news of the long-awaited loan on our home or our baby had survived major surgery, he said, "This is your lucky day, Judy. That was my boss. He saw you come into the office and thinks you have such modeling potential that he wants to offer you a scholarship for the training program!"

"Lucky" caught my attention, but at the same time, I was surprised and a bit skeptical.

"This is the last scholarship available," he continued. "And he usually interviews someone first, but he just knew when he saw you that you'd be perfect for the program."

I was twenty-seven, surely old enough not to fall for such a line. But something overrode my good sense as I remembered myself as a young girl who was never convinced I was pretty, despite boyfriends, girlfriends, and family members telling me otherwise. Now, I was a girl from a small town in Iowa who was about to appear on major magazines across the country advertising major brands. My head was swimming with the possibilities as I signed my name on the dotted line, committing to the cost of the sixteen-week training program, minus the generous scholarship. I couldn't wait to tell my family and friends.

Telling them had the totally opposite effect of what I expected. No one believed the training program would do anything but take my money and dash my hopes. When I got to the part about the timely phone call from the owner offering me the amazing scholarship, I noticed the scowls on their faces and their raised eyebrows. After many of these looks from people I trusted, I was convinced I'd been duped.

I called my brother, Don, an attorney. He asked lots of questions, especially about the form I signed for the financial commitment, but he never said, "How could you do something so stupid?" He didn't have to. By that time, I was saying it to myself loud and clear. Don told me the contract needed to be declared null and void on the basis of false pretenses and promises. He would prepare a document to be signed by me and the man I had dealt with at the agency.

When I called the interviewer at the modeling agency, his friendliness and enthusiasm made delivering the news of canceling my contract almost unbearable. He acted stunned that I could refuse the amazing offer that would change my life. I held firm and said I was prepared to bring my attorney to the agency if there were any problems.

There was no resistance. He signed, I signed, and my modeling career was over before it even began.

North Beach

*Someone pick me up
the old man yelled
as three people stepped
over him.
Help me he said
as I walked by.
I asked twice he said
as I returned
with one hand extended.
What do you need?
I need to get up.
We lifted—both of us.
A broken heap of mud
and old dreams.
He stood with nowhere
to go and sat back down again.*

King's Dream, My Nightmare

MARTIN LUTHER KING, JR. WAS SHOT and killed in 1968 as he stood on the second-floor balcony outside his room at the Lorraine Hotel in Memphis, Tennessee. I was devastated by his assassination and later by the Vietnam War and the protests against it. Soon after King's demise, I left my job as a social worker in Kansas City, Missouri. I headed to Iowa to see my brother Joe, who was attending university in Iowa City. The campus there and in many college towns was turned upside down with anti-war demonstrations, and I joined in. I wanted to participate in all of it.

After leaving Iowa, I made several stops across the country to visit former college friends. When I heard there was a memorial march in Jackson, Mississippi, to honor the anniversary of King's assassination, I wanted to be part of it.

I made friends with Roger, a Black man, at the march, and when it ended, he offered to drive me to the Mississippi River to give me my first glimpse of the mighty waters. We had planned to meet up with his friends afterwards for pizza.

We drove down a narrow, dusty road that led to Roger's favorite spot by the river. It was dark and isolated. I looked out the back window and saw headlights. I wondered who was in the cars and why they were following us so closely.

The two cars stopped a few feet behind ours and turned off their headlights. Four Mississippi state policemen got out and surrounded our car. They yelled at Roger. "Get out of the car, nigger." Then they reached inside, pulled him out, and dragged him away.

"What are you doing with this nigger? Do your parents know where you are?" one of the others shouted at me.

I was twenty-nine, terribly naive, and so I told the officer the truth: I was on a solo adventure and had told no one where I was, not even my parents.

"Let's have your driver's license." I handed it over, and the officer walked back to his partner. I stared straight ahead at the Mississippi as I heard them calmly suggest a plan. "Hell, she's traveling alone. No one knows where she is. We could tear up her license and throw them both in the river. Who would ever know?"

Images of my life flashed before me. I saw my parents, brothers, sisters, friends—all the people I'd known, all the people I loved, all the people who loved me. I saw myself at the bottom of the river, my long blonde hair flowing in the water. Would my body rise to the top? Would rocks be required to keep it on the bottom? How long does it take to drown? Would drowning bloat my body?

My mind was in free fall. Who would find me? Instinctively, I knew I needed to stay calm. Two things would help me to do that: surrender to what was happening and remember the people who loved me.

The policeman came back to the car and handed me my driver's license. "If you know what's good for you, you'll never be seen with a nigger in this town again. It's just not what we do here."

Roger returned to the car, limping and coughing up blood. The police drove away, leaving a trail of dust behind.

I asked Roger if he was okay to drive.

"I'm okay," he said as he drove away from the river.

After the police left and I felt safer, I got in touch with all my fear and outrage. "We need to tell someone what just happened! We need to report this, Roger!"

He looked at me, a blank stare on his bruised face, and I understood. Report it to whom? The police who had just beaten him and threatened to throw us both in the Mississippi?

I thought of the poster I'd seen on the ground at the march with words from Dr. King's final speech: I Have a Dream. It was covered with dirt, footprints, and food and drink stains, ready to be swept away. A nightmare.

What I Know About the Ocean

MY MOTHER WAS MESMERIZED BY THE ocean when she saw it for the first time during a trip to visit me when I lived in San Diego. She stood silent before the waves as we watched them ebb and flow, sometimes gently lapping the shore, other times breaking wildly and noisily in the near distance. Mom loved it all.

I was glad to see her happy and content. She had experienced depression much of her life. I loved seeing that heavy fog lift from her and knew the sense of relief she must have felt based on my own episodes of depression.

The ocean is where I wanted to go after my father died. My husband, Tony, picked me up from the airport after I returned to California from Iowa, where I had attended Dad's funeral and his burial in the local cemetery in Carroll, where Dad had lived his entire life.

I needed the vastness of the sea and the sprawling sky to resurrect Dad in California. We immediately went to the ocean. No other place would do. Not a church or a cemetery or my home. I was convinced I'd find Dad in the power and constant movement of the ocean waves and the immense sky above, and somehow be able to communicate with him. I was right. The ocean contained him, held him for me, and understood in a way no human being could. The strong, indelible mark he left on me and the sorrow would eventually transform into the life energy to go on after my North Star was gone.

Jeff's Kidnapping

THE YOUNGSTERS LINED UP IN ROWS for our usual morning walk to the school, a block away from the daycare center where their parents had dropped them off and where Janet and I worked. Jeff, a thin and fidgety kid, was in the back of the line. We had just started our walk when a car drove up and onto the sidewalk, startling us and preventing us from moving ahead. The driver, an adult male, quickly grabbed Jeff and pushed him into the car.

I was at the front of the line. Janet was at the rear and had a better view of the man hastily plucking Jeff out of our well-organized line. She threw her body against the car, pounded the door with her fists, and yelled, "Jeff, get out of the car!!" This was a kidnapping, and her powerful thrusts and high-pitched yelling signaled her serious intention that this would not happen on her watch.

I was impressed and amazed at the force of her reaction, but never once thought of joining in her vehement protest. I stood observing the scene carefully and realized how useless it would be to throw my body against the car to demand Jeff's release, too. The driver of the car sped away with a startled Jeff in the passenger seat. I watched him go, busy recording every detail in my mind's eye.

The kids were all abuzz.

"Ms. Judy, what happened?"

"Who took Jeff?"

"Where is that man taking Jeff?"

And then the worst possible question: "Could that happen to us, Ms. Judy?"

With the calmest voice I could manage, I assured them, "Everything is okay and we're here to watch over you." By that time, the police had arrived, which added immeasurably to my empty reassurance that the kids were safe with Janet and me. After all, Jeff had just disappeared in a quick minute in front of all of us.

We returned to the daycare center and called parents to inform them of the disruption to our routine. Jeff's abduction had traumatized the children, and it was best if their parents picked them up as soon as possible.

The officer assigned to investigate the kidnapping approached me and asked if I would write my observations of what had taken place, creating a document the police department could use to crack this case of a stolen child.

The enormity and importance of such a task filled me with laser-beam energy, enough to guide me in recording every detail I observed of the abduction. I was glad I hadn't rushed to attack the assailant's car as Janet had done. I had remained quiet and steady, allowing my mind to record as many details as I could remember.

The officer gave me a form with some guiding questions, and I dove into the writing as if this was my time, my hour to shine. I could see it all happening in my mind and recorded all the details as they unfolded. I wrote quickly without censoring my words. A freedom related to the importance of the task carried me through. I handed the paperwork to the officer. He was demonstrably pleased with what I'd written and assured me it would help with the investigation. That word "investigation" rang a loud bell that reverberated through my entire body. This was a day like no other.

Later, the investigation revealed that the man who had stolen Jeff was his father. The parents had separated and were fighting over custody of the boy. A restraining order forbade the father from visiting Jeff at home. He knew Jeff's daily routine of walking to school in a line from the day care center and hatched a plan to abduct him then. Police found him and Jeff, and returned Jeff, unharmed, to his mother.

It had been an exciting day for everyone. When Jeff returned to daycare, the kids had many questions about what had happened. He'd never been a popular kid, but he was in the spotlight after this experience!

As I look back, the thrill of being asked to record the details of the kidnapping has stayed with me along with the police officer's appreciation for the help I provided in solving a mystery. I'm now a Historical Detective/Family Historian with the same desire to solve family mysteries by carefully listening to stories of daily life and recording every detail. I have the observation and recording of Jeff's abduction to thank for lighting a fire that has never gone out.

Providential

LIKE ANGELS OF MERCY, MOM, MY sister Linda, and I drove to see my mother's sister. Sister Barbara Ann was dying from cancer at Villa St. Joseph, the hospital of the Sisters of Perpetual Adoration in LaCrosse, Wisconsin. The Villa was just up the hill from the motherhouse, Saint Rose Convent, where my aunt had first joined the community of nuns. We'd never been to the Villas before but were familiar with Saint Rose Convent where, when we were young, we visited Sister Barbara frequently with our grandparents. We arrived late. It was getting dark, and a heavy mist covered the grounds. It was like pulling up to a large haunted house.

Nevertheless, we were greeted cordially by the good sisters and led to the rooms the nuns had prepared for our stay. Mom took one room, and Linda and I took the other. My sister and I have a history of being poor sleepers, but that night as we yakked, we both fell asleep mid-sentence. We later agreed that we should do this more often because it might cure our sleep issues.

Sister Barb was aware we were there, but her eyes were closed when we went to her room in the morning. Mom and Linda made a beeline for her arms, took them gently in their hands, and began rubbing them as if they'd secretly trained as physical therapists or hospice nurses. I looked on in awe, feeling inadequate and lost as they easily slipped into their helping roles.

Several days later, our cousin, Gary Hausman, arrived with his wife and two adult daughters. They'd driven a long way in hopes of seeing Barb before she died. Gary was very fond of her. Barb lay still in her bed, her eyes closed, as they'd been the whole time we'd been at her side. Gary walked into the room and greeted her with his strong, booming voice.

"Hey there, Sister Barb."

She immediately recognized his voice. Her eyes popped wide open and stayed that way the entire time he was there. Although she couldn't speak, Barb grabbed onto his arm and held as tightly as she could.

Barb's given name was Zelma, but when she chose to enter the convent, it was changed to Sister Barbara Ann. She was well-educated and, for a time, she taught math at the high school in Carroll. When I was home from college, we'd meet for lunch at a local cafe. She was always interested in what I was learning, and she was always learning herself, attending numerous seminars to improve her many math skills.

The nuns caring for Sister Barb had no idea how long she would live. We were conflicted about leaving and kept asking the nuns for their opinion. It could be days or weeks before Sister Barb was ready to let go. With such uncertainty, my mom, Linda, and I decided to leave, a day after Gary had left. We gave Barb lots of kisses and loving goodbyes, and thanked the nuns for taking such good care of her.

For old times' sake, we decided to stop by Saint Rose Convent, down the hill from the Villa. We'd visited Barb there many times with our grandparents when we were kids, and had fond memories of the nuns' hospitality.

I dropped off Linda and circled the block. Mom stayed in the car with me. When I pulled up to the front of the motherhouse, Linda was standing with a distinguished-looking nun sporting a cane. Linda waved excitedly, as if she had something very important to say. Turns out, the nun had just gotten word that Barb died a few minutes after we left her. If we hadn't stopped at the motherhouse before leaving La Crosse, we wouldn't have known until we got home. We were shocked at the timing and puzzled over how this had happened. We had thought, and the nuns had confirmed, that Sister Barb could hold on for a while.

The nun at the motherhouse seemed to read our minds. She stood tall, positioned her cane, and uttered a word Linda and I never forgot and always used when other surprising phenomena like this happened in our lives.

"Providential," she said. "Providential."

Instinct

I HOPED THAT EVERYTHING WITH OUR water-damaged house was going to work out. One good sign: I turned my calendar to February and read the quote: "In the darkest hour, may light break through."

About the same time, the lights in the kitchen, which had stopped working the night before, came back on. My husband and I were ready to call an electrician when my intuition kicked in. The large fan the workers had brought in to dry out the water damage to our laundry room from the leaking water heater might have something to do with the lights going out. Voila! That was the problem, despite what Brandy at the repair company said. She had her doubts but gave me permission to unplug the fan. Immediately, the lights came back on. Maybe, I thought, I should get into this line of work—troubleshooting home repair problems!

It felt good to have lights again and to have solved this problem without calling an electrician. Tony hadn't quite trusted my idea about the connection between the fan and the lights, but had to admit, once it worked, it was a genius insight.

It's not so much about this particular problem with the lights but more of an encouragement to trust my instincts and follow through with what seems the right thing to do in my daily life. Trusting my gut *is* the right thing to do, but there are innumerable times when I stop myself or hold back from expressing what I'm feeling or sense I know. I want to remember this day and how my intuition guided me to the right solution. It could help me a great deal in other aspects of my life.

Heating Up

WITH RECORD-BREAKING TEMPERATURES ACROSS THE GLOBE, I've asked myself what I can do in the face of worsening climate change news. Study after study confirms that the planet has not been this hot in at least a thousand years, possibly longer.

Images in the news of people sweltering in such extreme heat frighten and depress me. Not wanting to remain in that dark space, I turn to my usual sources of solace—writing about my thoughts and reading books that offer added awareness and possibly hope.

The first book I turned to was not exactly reassuring, but it was very enlightening: *The Heat Will Kill You First: Life and Death on a Scorched Planet* by Jeff Goodell. It was published at the same time the heat was literally scorching many places on Earth. Goodell has written about climate change for years and was in Phoenix, Arizona, when temperatures soared to 117 degrees for several consecutive days. As he tells it, he was walking down a sidewalk in Phoenix when he experienced lightheadedness, rapid heartbeat, and elevated blood pressure. The symptoms led him to a detailed study of how our bodies react to temperatures over 95°F. It's not good news, and it got my attention.

I grew up with high heat and humidity. My siblings and I dealt with it by frequenting the American Legion swimming pool in our small Iowa town. Our parents provided us with swim lessons and a season ticket to the pool every summer. We stayed in the pool so long our skin became puckered, but it became our daily refuge from the worst of the heat. At night, when temperatures soared, we positioned a large fan and trays of ice cubes in our upstairs bedroom window to blow over us; a crude but innovative form of air conditioning. When our homemade air conditioner didn't provide enough relief to sleep, we grabbed our blankets and pillows and headed out to our front yard to sleep under the stars. Despite pesky mosquitoes and other summer bugs, the slight breeze outside allowed us a few hours of shuteye.

The heat that Goodell and other writers refer to is different. The addition of climate warming to hot summer weather has greatly worsened the effects of heat. We weren't expecting to see these disastrous effects so soon, but now we see people suffering from the effects of high heat in Arizona, Texas, and many other places in the US, Europe, and other nations. The entire globe seems to be on fire, and, sadly, people are dying from the extreme heat.

I live in the Bay Area of California and enjoy our 70° temperatures. But hearing constant updates of sizzling temperatures in other parts of the world, I know temperatures in the Bay Area are likely to rise.

What do coal, oil, and gas executives think as they watch people suffering from rising temperatures? It must not matter to them, or they convince themselves it's just a natural weather pattern. They misled us for decades about what they knew to be true as carbon accumulated in our atmosphere. They claimed the evidence was not clear or strong enough to discontinue the use of fossil fuels they knew were destroying the planet. If we take off our blinders and face the truth, we see clear evidence of the deadly effects—fires, floods, rising sea levels, and rising temperatures among them—for life on the planet if we continue to rely on fossil fuel extraction for our energy needs.

As the question, "What can I do?" nags at me, I think of what I've done in the past to show my objection to problems in the world. I was lucky enough to attend a small Catholic girl's school in the Midwest in the 1960s where my social work mentor and guide, Sister Francis Therese, a firebrand of a woman, exposed us to the many social problems of the time and encouraged us to follow the lead of Dr. Martin Luther King Jr. to march and protest for civil rights and any rights being ignored by society. She beamed when she knew we'd been out there making our objections known.

I'm in awe of Greta Thunberg and the beginnings of her one-woman stand against climate change, which has now sparked the souls of so many and grown into an international movement. I read of Extinction Rebellion members gluing themselves to buildings and roads to draw attention to the climate crisis. Although I can't imagine gluing myself to anything, I still hear the voice of Sister Frances Therese urging me to make my objections known and believe that actions can create change, as they did in the sixties. We made a national commitment then and allocated money for change.

We're in a very different time now. With the dangerous polarization of people across the globe, there appears to be no consensus on how to deal with the serious problems we're facing. With so many divisions and conflicts, we don't seem capable of creating the life-affirming programs we need. But this is the time we have, the time we've been given.

Sister Francis Therese might encourage us to do something small that brings us satisfaction, whether that's sending money to support climate change groups or signing petitions. Perhaps gluing yourself to buildings to disrupt the status quo and draw attention to the severity of the crisis is your thing. There's plenty to do, both big and small, and we have a lot of company.

I often think of the devastating fires in Maui in 2023. At the same time, climate-denying programs have been approved as part of the state curriculum in Florida. Perhaps, as Buddhist scholar Pema Chodron writes in her book, *When Things Fall Apart,* "It's time to have a cup of tea with chaos." And perhaps with the tea, a book that might offer a sliver of hope to face and soothe our sorrow, anger, fear, and dismay at the reality of climate change.

Below, I offer some books that I've found to be helpful and of possible benefit. Fortunately or unfortunately, many more are out there, and many more are likely to be written.

Not Too Late: Changing the Climate Story from Despair to Possibility edited by Rebecca Solnit & Thelma Young Lutunatabua. Solnit has decided to pull back from other writing and focus exclusively on writing about the climate crisis.

How to Live in a Chaotic Climate by Laura Schmidt, Aimee Lewis Reau, and Chelsie Rivera. This book offers ten steps from the Good Grief Network to foster resilience in a chaotic climate. Examples of the steps range from accepting the severity of the predicament to taking breaks and resting.

A Field Guide to Climate Anxiety: How to Keep Your Cool on a Warming Planet by Susan Jaquette Ray. I strongly identify with and appreciate the reference to "climate anxiety" in her title.

Falter: Has The Human Game Begun to Play Itself Out? by Bill McKibben. McKibben has written many books about the warming of the planet and what that may mean for life on earth.

The Heat Will Kill You First: Life and Death On a Scorched Planet by Jeff Goodell. Thoughtful, detailed, informative analysis of the effects of heat exacerbated by climate warming. Jeff's book is not entirely scary, and he reminds us we're all in this together.

Perhaps the stories gathered here can, as Rebecca Solnit says in her title, change the climate story from despair to possibility. I sincerely hope so for the sake of future generations.

The End of It

What did you do today? he asked.
I stared at the clouds she said.

Are you crazy?
No, are you?

I wanted you to sit and get fat.
I can't do it your way.

Then why are we together?
I thought I might go crazy.

Write it down he said.
I don't know what to say.

Say what you feel.
I haven't felt in years.

Maybe it's all wrong.
Maybe it's all right.

How can we know?
We can't, we can only feel.

But you haven't felt in years.
That's why I stare at the clouds.

What can you see?
Nothing, only myself.

But you must live and work.
I lived and it didn't work.

I'm afraid for you.
I'm afraid for me too.

What will you do?
The clouds will tell me.

You've gone off the deep end.
I wondered when I'd get there.

Where will you go now?
Over—without you.

The Scar

IN 2005, I WAS DIAGNOSED WITH and treated for cancer of the appendix, a very rare disease. Then, in 2012, it recurred, and I had an almost twelve-hour surgery that left a long scar from my breastbone to my groin. They opened me up to remove twenty pounds of fluid that had accumulated in my abdomen. The medical staff referred to this surgery as MOAS—the mother of all surgeries.

My husband, Tony, and I were traveling in Europe as the cancer was growing. We were in Amsterdam, the last stop on our family history journey, when a photo taken of me from the side revealed a bulging abdomen. I was startled. We'd been walking a lot throughout our trip, and I figured I should look trim.

The idea of cancer drifted ever so slightly through my consciousness, but I pushed the thought of recurrence out of my mind. After all, I'd taken Xeloda, a chemotherapy pill, for six months, and my oncologist had used the word "cured" when my treatment ended. Periodic bloodwork and annual CT scans confirmed the cancer had not returned.

But it had, without my knowledge, until the bulging abdomen photo showed evidence that something was not right. When we returned to Oakland, doctors drained the fluid from my abdomen. They suspected appendiceal cancer. Test results later confirmed the diagnosis. My cancer had metastasized.

Friends suggested that new treatments might have been discovered since 2005. My disease was so rare that I suspected nothing new had been developed. So little was known about cancer of the appendix that they used the same treatment as for colorectal cancer. I ended up in a colorectal support group because there were no specific groups for my type of cancer. Any time doctors heard I had appendix cancer, they'd say, "Oh, I've only read about that type of cancer. It's very rare. I've never really met anyone with it." I felt like a rock star and a freak at the same time.

Despite its rarity, there was a new treatment for my cancer if it metastasized to the abdomen. The experts were in La Jolla, California, so Tony and I flew there as soon as we could to consult with them.

The night before seeing Dr. Lowy, I did not sleep one wink. I spent the night doing meditation, tai chi, anything to support the health of my body. Filled with doubts and fears, I wondered if my case was an anomaly—something that couldn't be fixed. For the second time, I faced the prospect that I might die from this disease.

The specialist we met in La Jolla looked like movie star Jeff Chandler. Luckily, he was not only handsome but skilled. The frosting on the cake was his kindness. He said if I'd been unusually tired during our trip in Europe, it was because I was carrying twenty to twenty-five pounds of fluid in my abdomen. He took my hand, held it, looked me in the eyes, and said, "We can help you." I will never forget the sound of his voice and the touch of his hand on mine. Panic and doubt subsided, and my body relaxed. I knew I was in good hands. He explained the details of the operation to remove the cancerous fluid and any organ touched by cancer. The long, complicated process of undergoing the surgery was daunting, but it could save my life. I was ready to do whatever he asked.

With recovery time, we planned to be in La Jolla for three or four weeks. We made arrangements for someone to stay with our dog, Ruby. Tony stayed in a motel close to the hospital. Kaiser, our health care provider, covered all expenses and provided a per diem for Tony. We called our family and friends, and Tony promised to let them all know when I was out of surgery.

Early on a morning in September—it was Rosh Hashanah, the Jewish New Year—Tony took me to be admitted for the procedure. I hoped it was an auspicious date. The last thing I remember is saying goodbye to Tony and seeing the faces of the anesthesiologist and my surgeon.

Tony was unable to contact my family and friends right after I got out of surgery because he came to the recovery room too soon and saw me in such pain that I was moaning and pulling at all the tubes attached to me. A nurse finally assured him he could go back to the motel and return in the morning when I'd be in much better shape.

She was right. When he returned, I was completely drugged and sitting in a chair, smiling. I did everything the nurse asked me to do, from getting out of my chair to walking and sitting back down. I couldn't keep from grinning, even laughing, I felt so good. The drugs were doing what they were supposed to do.

The days that followed were not so pleasant. The drugs kept me fairly happy but also made me constipated. The food, except for the yogurt, was unappetizing. My sleep was constantly interrupted for taking my vitals. I'd open my eyes and see a team of doctors studying me. I became so sick of them that I finally got a computer from social services so I could watch movies and ignore the never-ending stream of doctors.

I felt like I'd been hit by a Mack truck, even with the painkillers they gave me. Every night, I fibbed to the nurse about my level of pain so she would give me more of the wonder drug that sent me quickly and deeply to dreamland. When I was ready to be discharged after my three-week stay, they gave me a healthy supply of painkillers and other prescriptions to take home with me. When I spotted the surgeon in the hospital hallway, I said, "Thank you for saving my life." He shrugged and said, "That's what we're here for." His response seemed blasé to me, considering the enormity of the event.

Once home, Ruby greeted me with kisses, and I knew this was where my true healing would take place. I lay on the sofa, waiting for my strength to return, and she stayed by my side, watching over me. Friends came to visit, and Tony tried to fatten me up with delicious meals, although I couldn't bear to eat right away.

When I was well enough to be up and about, the hospital staff asked me to serve as a mentor/coach for others who had had the same surgery. I got to know and support Gladys, who was encouraged by how well I was doing.

Another young woman who was about to have the surgery asked, "Will the scar show? Do they use invisible thread?" I was of little use to her, for I had not thought about the scar that covered half my body. I was alive, and that's what mattered most.

Easy Transition

WHEN MY HUSBAND AND I RECEIVED the call from our landlady, Susan, telling us she was selling the house we'd been living in for twenty-plus years, the house we planned to die in, all I could say was, "Oh, my God, oh my God."

The rent was $700 per month, an incredible deal in the increasingly hot Bay Area housing market. We hardly ever complained or asked Susan to pay for upkeep or repairs. Deferred maintenance became a way of life for us, and she kept the rental price low. Many people in the Bay Area did this to cope with the nightmare of rising rents and home sale prices. We probably carried it to an extreme.

We had one wall heater in the living room for our 990-square-foot house, and we often wore down jackets inside during the winter months. When peeling paint on the exterior became an embarrassment, we hired a friend to paint, and Susan agreed to cover half of the expense. Susan thought we would want to buy the house when she was ready to sell. We considered it and went so far as to hire inspectors to come and take a good look. Early on, it was clear they were looking at the house with different eyes than we had for twenty years. They were unimpressed by the views of the expanse of trees bordering an open meadow, which were visible the moment you walked into the house. There were also plenty of trees on the sides of the house, so we never felt crowded by neighbors.

The living room lent itself to big dinners and celebrations. Our family and friends relished sitting on the couch while watching the sun go down. For a time, Tony and his catering team set up party trays in our living room and kitchen to prepare for large events. When Ruby, our Norwich Terrier, turned six, our neighbors and friends crowded into the living room and filled the front porch and part of the yard to celebrate with us. I used my finest Martha Stewart decorating tricks to cover up any obvious signs of wear and tear. At night, I kept the lamp lights low.

It all worked until the inspectors came. They had a tear-it-down look in their eyes, trying to gauge if any part of the house was salvageable. They moved furniture, exposing problem areas in the house that we had never paid attention to. They found dry rot and mold that we'd carefully kept a blind eye to all those years. They weren't interested in our front yard, brimming with flowers and plants, or the crabapple tree, now in full bloom, that my mother-in-law had given us. Their reports were filled with all the bad news we'd expected but refused to deal with. We'd been outed; the defects of the house written up like an F grade in primary school that we could no longer gloss over. It was brutal and costly.

But that didn't mean I was ready to leave. I hid in my room and worked on family history projects rather than joining Tony in the search for a new house. Neither he nor anyone else was going to make me leave my home, even if it was looking more and more like a shack. Tony wondered what I thought was going to happen. Were we going to end up living on the streets?

One day, up to his neck in frustration, Tony picked up a flyer for a house for sale and begged me to look at it with him. I agreed. The house he'd found was close by, down the hill, and in the same zip code. It was within walking distance to Farmer Joe's market, where we'd been shopping for twenty years.

It had an unusual look on the outside after a makeover by *Curb Appeal* a few years before. The moment we stepped into the house, we both knew it was our new home. Light from the many windows made me aware that the trees we'd enjoyed for years in our old home had been obscuring the light.

I had to admit our house of twenty years was dark, dare I say even foreboding? Hadn't our neighbor Jack once called it a shack long before the inspectors came? He, of course, refers to the famous Jack London family, who had bought the house years before when it was surrounded by orchards. When developers bought the land for the subdivision, the Londons agreed to the sale of everything but the house they had lived in. Maybe they were attached to that house for the same mysterious, sentimental reasons I was.

Tony and I walked through our prospective home, enjoying the light dancing against the walls in every room and marveling at the features of the house, including central heating. The owners had done an extensive remodel and paint job, all in good taste. They expanded the kitchen as if they knew a chef was moving in and installed an O'Keefe & Merritt gas stove. For me, there was the breakfast nook where I could relax and keep Tony company as he cooked our dinners.

Red bougainvillea bloomed wild in the back yard, reminding me of what I'd seen years before at another house. I had filed that image away until I saw it again and realized it was something I'd cherish in my life.

We finished our tour and stepped outside. There were sidewalks, dogs on leashes, children in strollers, and beautiful trees. The neighborhood was perfect for walking Ruby and riding bicycles.

Later, when we wrote a letter to the sellers telling them why we wanted to buy the house, we mentioned the central heating, the hardwood floors, and the new stove, the bougainvillea, and much more. The owners accepted our bid. How had this seemingly perfect house appeared in our lives when I was filling my mind with all the doubts and worries of moving? I will recall this easy transition when I go through the next one and the doubts and worries slip in and make me fearful of leaving the familiar for the unknown—in this case, the wonderful new home we've been fortunate to live in for a dozen years.

The Nunnery

SLEEP DEPRIVATION CONSUMED ME UNTIL MY mother-in-law, Rosi, invited me to join her on a restorative vacation in the mountains of Mexico. The lack of sleep was affecting me in ways I didn't think possible. I was unsure I could even organize, pack, and get to Mexico. But Rosi mentioned that in addition to the spa, there was a nunnery nearby with nuns who dispensed healing herbs to care for the sick. That gave me the needed energy to go.

My plane arrived in Guadalajara, where a taxi driver was waiting to take me to Rio Caliente. We drove swiftly on the main highway and then moved at a slow crawl over the cobbled streets of La Primavera, the small town at the foot of the mountain. I immediately spotted a cow in a side yard of one of the small stucco homes. Two roosters crossed our path, followed by several dogs. It was early morning, and the town was slowly waking up, the perfect introduction to a completely different world.

We began our ascent of the mountain into the pine forest. Numerous potholes forced the driver to go even more slowly, allowing me to relax and take in the beauty and fresh fragrance of the Sierra Madre Mountains.

A hearty-looking man named Harold met me and the taxi driver at the gate. I later learned Harold was eighty-three, and he and his seventy-nine-year-old wife, Esther, would be the activities directors during our stay. They were getting ready to lead a group, including Rosi, on a hike. Later in the day, they taught yoga and tai chi. I declined the walk and had the driver take me to my room, where I could set up my journals and books and make the room my home for the week. Large windows opened out onto a magnificent view of the mountains, and a breeze cooled the room to a perfect temperature.

Rosi joined me after the hike and told me of the many activities we could sign up for, but first, she wanted to make plans to visit the nunnery. Rosi's physical problems and my problem with sleeplessness made it an important destination.

The nunnery was close, outside the gates to the spa, and Sister Glory, who had been highly recommended, met people between four and five each evening. She was an iridologist and prescribed medication based on the problems she saw when she looked in your eyes. She spoke in Spanish but, luckily, Pilar, a Spanish-speaking guest, would be joining us to translate.

Pilar introduced us to Sister Glory, who was working out of what looked like a dark, windowless, abandoned shack with flies everywhere. Nuns were preparing mud packs for the thin, bandaged patients, who were seated and lying on benches.

This place was referred to as the home for the sick. I noticed the fourteen Stations of the Cross with images of Christ attached to wood on the walls. There were wildflowers in a coffee can placed on an altar honoring the Virgin Mary. Vials of herbs and simple crucifixes were abundant. Despite the crudeness of the place, I stopped noticing the flies and focused on the peace and love that surrounded us as we watched the nuns ministering to the patients.

After looking in my eyes with a small flashlight, Sister Glory told me that many people came for help with sleeplessness, and she had no more of her herbal remedy left. With disappointment in her voice, she asked me to return the next day. We arrived early the next day and were thrilled to hear the nuns' lovely, light voices singing their prayers. Sister Glory was happy to see us, but again said we could not get the remedy. She had the liquid remedy but no containers to put it in. The containers were being sent from the motherhouse in Guadalajara. Could we come back? We laughed and said we could.

Pilar had come with us again, and the sister told her something that Pilar later translated. Sister Glory had been diagnosed with brain cancer five years before. Her doctor had said there was no treatment and she would die from the cancer. Instead, she ingested herbs, used mud wraps, took cold baths, and ate raw vegetables—all the remedies the nuns used on the patients who came to see them. Her tumors were oozing out and shrinking, she said, as she pointed to the bandages just under the cap of her white nun's habit.

Everything now seemed surreal as I became aware I was in another culture and bearing witness to something strange and mysterious with the treatment that appeared to be keeping Sister Glory alive.

I wasn't able to go to the nunnery the day the remedy was ready. Pilar agreed to pick it up for me. I busied myself with packing and squeezing in one last massage and time in the sauna and pool. Before going to my room, I checked in on Rosi. We heard voices outside her door. I looked out and saw Pilar and Sister Glory. She was beaming with so much love, I immediately went out and hugged and kissed her. Rosi followed with a hug and kiss, unusual gestures for her.

Sister Glory had come in the dark of night, accompanied by another nun, to deliver the herbs she thought would help me with sleep. I loved her for doing that. Rosi and I both commented on how easy it was to hug and hold her, to give her more kisses as we said goodbye. Before she left, Sister Glory told Pilar she'd been to the doctor that day, and he confirmed that her tumors were still shrinking. He still does not understand it, and she continues to beam with love and feel hopeful.

I left the spa bearing no souvenirs except the precious items from Sister Glory: tila, salvia, cola de caballo, meliza, and liquid valerian. The herbs brought me rest, but they are long gone. Yet, the loving memory of Sister Glory at the nunnery remains.

Aunt Edith

EDITH WAS MY DAD'S OLDER SISTER. Although I knew her from graduation parties and other special events, Dad revealed the story of a special relationship I had with Aunt Edith. I learned about it during my early thirties, a troubling period in my life brought on by a lack of trust in the romantic relationship I was in and cutbacks in social services that added stress to my job as a social worker.

For years, my life had looked promising with work, relationships, and travel, but at some point, it all began to crumble, and I became depressed and unhappy. My parents knew I was suffering when I called and asked if they could tell me anything about my early life that may have been traumatic or shed light on my current troubles. They were both on the line and told me the story of my mother's nervous breakdown in 1944.

Mom was hospitalized for a month in Omaha, Nebraska, which is about a hundred miles from our home in Carroll.

"What we now know is it was probably postpartum depression after Mom gave birth to your younger sister Pat," Dad said.

I was three months shy of two years old when Mom was hospitalized. My dad had been inducted into the US Navy nine months before. With both parents gone, relatives stepped in to care for my two siblings and me. Dad told me that Aunt Edith and Uncle Carlos, who lived about sixty-five miles from our home, took care of me in their home in Boone, Iowa.

I was shocked. "What about Donnie? And Patsy?" I demanded, my voice shaking.

My older brother, Don (Donnie), was almost five, and my younger sister, Pat (Patsy), was three months old. Dad said Don stayed with Grandpa Vasos in his home. Mom's parents, Grandma and Grandpa Hausman, cared for Patsy on their farm ten miles away.

When Grandma Hausman died, the family discovered her diaries. Her daughter took them and, much later, gave them to me. The diaries added more information to this period of time. When Patsy was with Grandma, she was hospitalized because she couldn't keep her milk down. Grandma was not well, and it became too much for her to deal with these added troubles. The facts Dad revealed became more and more disturbing. Not only had we borne the separation from our parents, but we siblings were separated from each other as well.

It would take years of sleuthing to fill in the pieces of this story and years of therapy to befriend the little girl inside me who had felt lost and abandoned by what had happened.

Several years after Dad died, I was visiting my mother when I learned that Aunt Edith was in a nursing home, her health failing. It seemed the right time to visit and thank her for taking care of me. My mother agreed to come with me. I thought it might be disturbing for her to see Edith and relive this painful experience, but she said she wanted to go.

When we walked into Aunt Edith's room at the nursing home, she was in bed. When she saw us, she looked up, beamed, and reached out to us. She'd always been perky, and that aliveness was still evident in her face. We pulled up chairs next to her bed, and I reached for her hand. Before I had a chance to say one word, she looked at me intently and said, "I took care of you when you were very young. You were my little doll. I made dresses for you, and you were as cute as a button. I loved you so much."

Utterly astonished, I soaked in her words and said, "Oh, Aunt Edith, I came here to thank you for taking care of me. I didn't know about it until Dad told me the story several years ago." She gripped my hand tightly and tears welled up for both of us. "All the years I knew you, when you came to graduations and other family events, I had no idea that I lived with you when I was little. I never knew you'd cared for me, and I want to thank you now that I know."

The visit was short, but it was the right time for both of us to acknowledge the importance of the time we had with one another. When we returned home, Mom said she had something for me and brought out a beautiful blue crystal plate with matching cups and sugar and milk containers. It was the set they'd given Aunt Edith as a thank-you gift for taking care of me. She'd given it back to them when she moved to the nursing home. Mom wanted me to have it now.

A few months later, Aunt Edith slipped into a coma and died. She was eighty-six. I still ask myself how we both knew it was the right time to say those healing, grateful words to one another. That question may never be answered. All I can do is be thankful for the timing of all the events: to Dad for telling me the true story, to Mom for going with me to visit Aunt Edith, to Aunt Edith for staying alive long enough to tell me how special and memorable the experience of taking care of me was, and to be able to thank her for it.

Car Magic

HER NAME WAS ELLY, AND HER color was metallic grey, but she changed colors depending on the light. I liked that she was like a chameleon and that my friends had to ask every once in a while, "What color is she?" I thought I'd have Elly forever. She was brand new in 2011.

Oakland, California, is a designated high-crime area, but we live in a relatively safe neighborhood, according to the policeman who took the report when I told him my Elly had been stolen. She was parked, as always, right in front of our house. Five neighbors and I heard the car alarm go off. One neighbor estimated it was 3:00 a.m. None of us got out of bed to check out what was happening. I don't know about the others, but I didn't budge because I was afraid whoever was stealing Elly might pull a gun on me. I also thought there was no way it could be my Hyundai Elantra, a selfish thought in retrospect.

My husband, Tony, noticed the empty space where Elly had been parked when he got up for his early morning swim. He saw the broken glass from the driver's side window and greeted me with this shocking news as soon as he returned. I called the police to report the crime. An officer arrived immediately after my call, which shocked me almost as much as the car theft.

He gave me lots of tips about stolen cars and said I probably didn't want to get my car back. What? Are you kidding? My Elly! But as he described the terrible things she might endure with the thieves (ransacking, drugs, urinating inside), I changed my mind about wanting her back. The best outcome, he said, was a decent insurance settlement if they declared it totaled. I started thinking about the bumps and scratches she already had and the trashed condition in which she might be returned to me. It didn't take long to conclude it was time for a different, better-looking car.

My mechanic suggested a Smart Car, one of those little half-cars that you can easily imagine being smushed to death in if it were struck by another vehicle. To allay my fears, he told me Mercedes-Benz manufactured the car with an extra steel-reinforced mounting within the frame. My family was not so easily convinced of the safety features, and, along with several friends, told me outright they didn't like the idea of me in a Smart Car. One friend said it reminded her of a clown car in the circus.

Still, Smart Cars started appearing like magic when I was on walks in the neighborhood. Was this just the frequency illusion, aka the Baader-Meinhof effect, of noticing something more frequently after learning about it? Each time I saw one, I hailed the driver and conducted a short interview about the pros and cons of the car. Everyone I interviewed said the same thing: they loved the car, it felt safe enough for the freeway, and though there was no back seat or trunk, they had room for groceries and a dog, if they had one.

I loved all these reports and decided I would take my time and see what the universe had in store for me. Every time I saw a Smart Car, my heart would soar, and I considered it a sign that one was out there for me.

Of course, you can't just wait for magic to do its thing. I realized I had to do my part and check with car dealers, take test drives, and complete all the other time-consuming tasks that acquiring a car entails. As the weeks went by, I noticed I had not done one of those things. Simultaneously, I was reconsidering the looks of the Smart Car. One day, when I saw one drive by, I thought, *What an ugly car!*"

During an afternoon of running errands, I was close to my mechanic's shop and stopped in to say hello. We started talking, and I told him I hadn't had the energy to find a Smart Car. He surprised me by asking if I wanted to check out a car he had just repaired that was now for sale.

It was a four-door sedan, and a Hyundai like my stolen car, but newer, with low mileage, in pristine shape, and selling at a reasonable price. And it was white, the color I'd decided on after reading that it was easiest for other drivers to see and therefore safer on the road. It was smaller than the car I'd had, but not pudgy like a Smart Car. I fell in love with it.

The insurance company had declared my car totaled after it was found abandoned, missing front and back bumpers, trashed inside, just like the police officer had predicted, with stolen suitcases lying in the back seat to boot. I was offered more than enough to cover the cost of the Hyundai Accent.

It wasn't a Smart Car, but it had come to me so easily, so magically, I had to assume it was the Right Car. I took it for a test drive, thanked the universe, and proclaimed it my car.

Separation

I think someone smart

could have saved us

    from all this

You left early

in the morning for adventure

I stayed home

to plant flowers

we wouldn't see for months

If we had spent

more Sundays together

we would have seen

    those plants

needed more

    than one watering.

Magic in the World

"ALL RIGHT. I'M ALL PACKED AND ready to go. Uber should be here in ten minutes," I called out to Tony.

I'm hardly ever on time, but this trip was important, and I was giving it all the time it deserved. Sioux Falls, South Dakota, was our destination, where my nephew was getting married. After four years of not seeing my siblings and their families, we were all planning to be there. My sister Linda had died a few years before, but the rest of us, Don, Pat, Joe, Dave, and I would be there, along with many nieces and nephews and great-nieces and great-nephews—fifty-four family members in total.

The stakes were high for many reasons. I'd seen the red dresses that my shapely niece and great niece were going to wear to the wedding. I knew I couldn't compete with them, but managed to pull together an outfit that reflected ME.

I triple-checked to be sure I had everything with me. Something in the back of my mind prompted me to check an essential part of my outfit, a white, silky top that had slipped off a hanger and was lying on the closet floor like a discarded rag.

As I placed it into my suitcase, I whispered a sigh of relief and great thanks that my intuition was strong enough to tell me about this possible slip-up. Lucky me for working on accessing my intuition during all these years of self-discovery.

Because of rising COVID-19 rates, Tony and I wore double masks to the airport and on the two flights required to get us to South Dakota. Wearing two masks is more uncomfortable than one, but we were determined to be safe.

I didn't remove my masks until we parked our rental car in the hotel's parking lot. I looked in the mirror to fluff up my hair after the many hours it had been smushed by the straps of the mask. I almost fainted. My gums were exposed in two empty spaces at the bottom of my mouth! I'd left one of the most essential parts of my outfit at home: a stay plate that fit neatly in the space where my two bottom teeth had once been.

I'd adapted easily to the plate and had only forgotten to wear it once. The first time was when I met a man personally whom I had only been in email contact with. I learned later that he wrongly assumed from my emails that I was a very organized and serious person. One look at my two missing bottom teeth disavowed him of that notion, but we became good friends. We laughed often about that first meeting, and he ended up writing the foreword to my book about the Holocaust.

But now I was faced with the prospect of not one person but dozens of them at the wedding seeing the gap. I was sure I couldn't face them. Despite the frenzy in my mind, I was able to see a possible plan. FedEx could overnight a package with the stay plate, but I'd have to get it to their office in Oakland. I called their main office and learned they could overnight packages but only on weekdays. Luckily, It was Thursday. There was one FedEx office still open in Oakland that would accept a package for overnight mailing. It closed at five o'clock; it was four fifteen.

I had to act fast to make this happen. I remembered that Tony had given our neighbor, Natalie, a key to our house. The chances of her being able to get the stay plate to FedEx were slim, but I was desperate and had to try. I called Natalie and left an urgent message. I texted and emailed her and her partner, David, sounding more and more desperate. Finally, my cell phone rang. It was Natalie, full of empathy for my situation, saying she would gladly take my precious cargo to FedEx.

The next morning, the front desk called to tell me a package had arrived. I knew it was my missing plate. What an effing miracle, I said to myself.

Natalie later told me she had several serendipitous experiences with people when she went to mail my plate. She was unfamiliar with the location of the FedEx office, but some obliging person who recognized she was lost accompanied her to the office. And once there, another helpful FedEx employee who grasped the importance of getting the package out on time did everything in his power to quickly package the stay plate and get it on its way. Natalie described this as one of those moments when everything was lined up for success. It was just one of those meant-to-be moments in life, she said.

How life and the people in it can work to make something wonderful—almost magical—happen is still a mystery to me. I once heard that the definition of magic is cooperating with the universe. I love magic in my life and have honestly tried to cooperate with the universe to bring in as much of it as I can.

Thanks to Natalie, the people she encountered doing this good deed, and FedEx's overnight mailing service, I believe this was one clear example of life creating magic. I was grateful to the universe. I could laugh loudly, talk excitedly, and eat and drink heartily with everyone at the wedding with a mouth full of teeth.

Perfect Timing

WHEN OUR DOG, RUBY, WAS NEARING the end of her life, I pushed her in a stroller every day in our neighborhood. We often ran into our two-year-old neighbor, Jonah, who was also being pushed in a stroller by his parents. He always said hi, and sometimes when Ruby licked his hands or face, he'd burst into giggles. I loved it when that happened.

After Ruby died, I was walking with my husband, Tony, and we ran into Jonah in his stroller. He barely looked at me, and he didn't say his usual greeting. Seemingly, he didn't know who I was without Ruby in her stroller, and he'd never seen Tony before. I was crushed and had a strong impulse to explain that Ruby had died. When I bent down to his stroller, his mom, knowing what I was about to say, looked at me and cautioned, "Too young. He's much too young to understand."

Was this being overly protective? I wasn't sure, but she was his mother, so I honored her wishes and didn't mention that Ruby had died.

It was a year or two before I saw Jonah again. He had outgrown his stroller and was jumping up and down outside his house in what his dad reasoned was a sugar high after eating too much of his birthday cake. I felt lucky to be seeing him on his birthday and joined in the chaos with happy birthday cheers.

In the middle of his romp with his friends, Jonah looked at me intently and asked, "Did Ruby die?"

"Yes, she did." I answered, startled.

"I used to see you pushing her in the stroller when I was being pushed in my stroller. She was so little and cute, and she gave me kisses."

"Oh, I remember, Jonah. She loved you so much and so do I."

His acknowledgment of Ruby's death after all that time filled me with relief and sparked philosophical thoughts: Everything in its own time. There's a time for everything. Trust in the timing of the universe. Don't push things. Everything works out, even when it takes longer than you think it will.

Jonah had come to the realization of Ruby's death in his own time and way. His mom was right; I didn't need to tell him about Ruby when I thought I did. It had all worked out in the most perfect way. Standing there among the partygoers, I'd forgotten I was holding a small box of oranges I'd picked up at another neighbor's before I saw Jonah. As I turned to leave, he disturbed my reverie about perfect timing. "Judy, Judy, he shouted." I turned back to him, and he asked, "Are those oranges in the box?"

I was thrown off, expecting him to say something more about Ruby. Did he want some of the oranges? How could our final note be of oranges? Well, it was, and that had to be perfect too.

Our Luck with Mom

AFTER MOM PASSED, THE SOCIAL WORKER at the local Alzheimer's Association suggested we have an autopsy of Mom's brain. This social worker had helped us through much of Mom's dementia. My sisters and I had suspected Alzheimer's but had no real proof until the autopsy. I mean, why else would she greet us in the nursing home where she lived as if she hadn't seen us for months, when we'd seen her five minutes before? Why, when at a loss for words, which was often, would she make up words? Once, at the local A&W restaurant, which touts all-American food, she ordered a root beer float and blessed us for being there with her. Then she slammed her hand down on the table and announced, "And God bless the table!"

We often took her for a drive on our visits and passed by several mansions. She wondered how many people lived there. Were there children? How many? Her curiosity spread far and wide, and she entertained us endlessly. She had a sense of wonder and joy about everything and got a kick out of the things she noticed. She'd never been that lighthearted or clever before, and she seemed younger, more delighted with life.

We'd heard that people with Alzheimer's could become angry, even hostile. We saw none of that. There was, of course, the forgetfulness, but given Mom's propensity for depression throughout her life, forgetting seemed a good thing. She couldn't remember what she'd been depressed about. Her forgetting and our having to constantly repeat things continued, but it paled in relation to the words she made up and the many ways she had my sisters and me in stitches.

At an Alzheimer's meeting I attended, I reported Mom's jovial behavior, but no one in the group could identify with such an experience. Their loved ones were exploding in anger and refused to do what staff and family members asked.

Mom did some inappropriate things in the nursing home, like going into a neighbor's room and crawling into bed with her. Now that she's gone, what she did struck me as sweet and tender. Maybe she wanted the comfort of another body in bed with her. Maybe she thought she was nestling next to Dad or one of her kids. There were complaints about her behavior, and she was moved to a higher level of care where she could be kept from doing such things.

It was not a burden to visit Mom during this time. She was up for anything and joined us in any game we suggested. Most often, and memorable, was Take a Penny, a simple, fun game that delighted her and our extended family. My great-nephew still mentions this game when he talks about her.

Before Mom's body went to Sharp Funeral Home, she was taken to the hospital where they removed her brain for the autopsy. It did nothing to harm her looks. Everyone commented on how gorgeous she looked in the casket during the funeral services. Don, my sister Pat's old boyfriend, was part of the staff who prepared her body and applied the make-up which enhanced her flawless, beautiful skin. We'd chosen a short-sleeved top for her, and the watch she wore every day was on her wrist as if she might be ready for a visit or a drive to the A&W for another root beer float. Lucky for all of us, we were left with happy memories of our mom.

Spin Cycle

I'M A WALKER. I WALK EVERY day on the sidewalks in our Oakland neighborhood. I've gotten to know many families on these walks. I recognize their kids, their dogs, and their cats. I'm known to some as the mayor of the neighborhood.

When Tony and I talked about taking a vacation in Maui, I thought snorkeling seemed like a fine new adventure. We stayed in Napili Bay and outfitted ourselves with snorkeling gear from Snorkel Bob's in town. Snorkel Bob's had everything. I wanted to be completely prepared, so in addition to the goggles and fins, I bought a royal blue, rash guard, polyester shirt to protect me from the sun.

The store manager put my hair in a ponytail to avoid pulling my hair out by the roots when I adjusted my goggles. Thank goodness for her help. My hair is important to me. After all, my husband is bald and one of us must have hair!

Although I hadn't been in a pool or the ocean for thirty years, I felt ready to get on with it. Sporting all my gear, I walked confidently with Tony to the water's edge, where I thought it would be calm enough for a beginner snorkeler.

As I said, I'm a walker. I do well on terra firma.

As we began this new-to-us activity, Tony fell on his butt at the water's edge. He beckoned me to go out further into the water, but by that time, I was on my back. Then my stomach. Then my side. Then on my back again. A complete spin cycle! Tony tried to help me get upright, to no avail. A young girl came over to assist him, but the cycle was not over. I continued to spin.

Andrew, a strong, stocky, fully tattooed man who had seen my spin routine from the beach, came and held out a hand. I grabbed hold of it and finally stopped spinning as he lifted me out of the water and stayed with me until we reached my blanket.

He mentioned that there were some calmer waters behind the Safeway in Lahaina, right down the road. "My daughters always make fun of those waters," he remarked. "Say they're for babies."

I thanked him for saving my life and said those waters sounded perfect to me.

Soon, people stopped by my blanket to console me. One guy looked at Tony snorkeling out in the bay and asked, "Is that your husband out there?" I nodded yes.

"What's his age?"

"He'll be seventy-nine," I replied.

"Very good!" he said, giving a thumbs up for emphasis, an indication that Tony and I weren't both losers in the water.

Full of sympathy, his wife said, "It's just like being in a washing machine, isn't it?" She had described my experience to a tee.

I gathered all my great gear and stumbled up the sand beach, heading back to our room. I felt embarrassed as I passed other people on the beach, sensing the pity oozing from them. My first snorkeling attempt had ended so sadly. How would I ever recover from the humiliation?

Then I saw the young girl who had tried to help steady me in the water, along with Tony. "It's just like being in a washing machine, isn't it?" she remarked.

"That's exactly what another woman just said!" I told her.

And right there and then, I knew that part of my recovery would be to write a story about my experience being in a washing machine. Spin Cycle. Writing has helped me more than once in my life. It might do the trick again.

My See-Saw Mind

I WAITED PATIENTLY FOR THE MEDICAL technician to start my annual exam. I was nervous about the blood pressure reading. It had been steadily rising as I aged. I was on Cozaar, a blood pressure medication that seemingly kept it under control. Still, I worried that the dosage would be increased if my readings were not at an acceptable level.

The tech applied the blood pressure cuff and then swiped a device across my forehead to take my temperature.

"86.61. It's so low, I wonder what's wrong?" she said.

I assumed she was referring to a problem with the instrument and not my body temperature. Meanwhile, the blood pressure cuff signaled it was time to take the reading. The tech quickly lunged to turn off the machine but was so engrossed in the low temperature problem that she neglected to share the blood pressure readings with me.

"Oh, by the way, how's my blood pressure?" I asked her with the calmest voice I could muster.

Distracted by a new temperature gauge, she quickly spit out the numbers: 136 over 85, excellent numbers for me. She had little interest in my relief, and, with a pained look on her face as if she were about to fail a final exam, she took my temperature again with the new instrument.

I crossed my fingers and hoped for the best. It was a perfectly normal reading of 98.6.

Knowing my temperature and blood pressure were normal, I calmed down and hoped the next step, seeing my doctor, would go extremely well. She entered the room with her usual enthusiastic smile. I relaxed as she reached for her stethoscope to begin the exam.

A stethoscope always reminds me of playing doctor as a kid and pretending to listen to my younger sister's heartbeat, wearing my white doctor's coat and official-looking play stethoscope. I never heard anything as I carefully put the instrument to her little heart. My report was always good. "Everything is fine. You're perfectly okay," I'd say as I sent her on her way, repeating what my doctor usually told me.

But today, my doctor's words were alarming. She heard something through that stethoscope: a heart murmur. She'd been my doctor long enough to know I worry about anything unusual, so she immediately said, "This heart murmur is nothing to worry about."

Not to worry? A murmur in my heart? The only heart I have! It sounded ominous, dire. Could I die of a heart attack? Stroke? I struggled to keep these thoughts to myself and hide any hint of freaking out. I needed to get an echocardiogram. I wasn't familiar with the procedure, so, of course, I worried about it. She told me it was only to get a baseline reading of my heart. That didn't sound so serious, and when she told me I couldn't get an appointment for two months, things seemed even less serious. It couldn't be an emergency or even serious if I had to wait two months to be seen by an echo tech.

Next, she reviewed my blood test results and reported, "You have prediabetes," then quickly added, "but don't worry!"

Too late. I was already imagining daily insulin shots for the rest of my life and eventually having a toe or part of my leg removed as the diabetes went haywire. She brought me back to earth when she emphasized the "pre" and told me there was a class where I'd learn about ways to prevent the development of type 2 diabetes.

I called to make an appointment for the class. The first opening was in three months. The person who enrolled me said it was very popular and always filled to capacity. He had a jolly tone to his voice. Could it be that bad if he was jolly and the class was always full? Maybe this diagnosis was normal, at least for my eighty years. Maybe I was overreacting to everything. I looked for a level of peace and calm within myself.

I felt I was on a roller coaster ride; first up with worry and then down with reassurance that these conditions were normal. With a little mental brush-up, I felt I could easily handle my next stop: the X-ray department.

I'd fallen on a curb some months earlier and fractured the humerus bone of my right arm. With time, my smart arm miraculously knit itself back together while I waited, and I developed a fine appreciation for patience and the body's desire and ability to heal.

All was going well until my husband and I agreed to take care of our neighbor's dog, a white West Highland terrier named Dewey. We loved Dewey. He was cute and the best-behaved dog we'd ever known. We let him sleep with us in our bed. One night, I got up to use the bathroom. It was dark when I returned to the bedroom, and I didn't notice Dewey had moved over to the edge of my side of the bed. I got into bed, and his body threw me off balance. I fell to the floor.

I thoroughly examined my body the next day for any damage, and all I found was a bruise on my right leg. No bones sticking out, no pain. I thought I was fine, but as more and more people suggested getting an X-ray to make sure everything was okay, I began to think it was worth pursuing. "It will put your mind at ease," they said. "There's probably nothing wrong, but your worries could be alleviated." Everyone pegged me correctly as a champion worrier in need of reassurance. I followed their advice.

Once inside the X-ray room, the technician told me that, despite it being Friday, it was *his* Monday, and he wasn't happy about just starting the week. I wasn't getting a good vibe from him and wanted to tell him to zip it and keep his troubles to himself. The vibe got worse as he began taking the images. He carried on a constant banter of questions. "Does your arm hurt? How long ago did you fall? Did you have surgery on your arm? You're *sure* your arm doesn't hurt?"

Filled with nervousness, I asked him to stop asking me these types of questions—questions that convinced me he was seeing something wrong.

"Ah, it's just talk," he said. I take good pictures, and the doctor will tell you about your arm." A statement I took to mean there was definitely something wrong with my arm.

In my mind, I began crafting a letter to his superiors about this inappropriate exchange. I didn't want him to be fired, but I also didn't want other people subjected to words that would cause worry. When this torture was over, I bolted out of the x-ray room with a limp-wrist goodbye wave and a scowl on my face.

Two hours later, I received an email with the results of the X-ray: no new fracture, unchanged alignment. Everything was fine.

Heart murmurs and prediabetes were apparently normal conditions for my age group. I became aware of my overreaction to everything. I analyzed why my mind had kicked up so much "worry dust."

Is this how everyone's mind works? Is worrying what we *all* do in situations like this? Does my worry go over the top? Am I a worrywart? Possibly. Probably. My sister referred to this type of behavior as fretting and said we both had advanced cases. It was one of the "gifts" from our mother, an expert at fretting.

But over the years, worry had just brought on more worry, stress, and fretting. I'd grown tired of it and looked for ways to escape or at least reduce it. I wanted to lay this burden down and return to a saner way of dealing with life. After an emotionally draining morning, I used some of the tricks I'd learned.

I stepped outside and saw the most beautiful, red-orange, smoky-blue Arizona-style sunset. It completely washed over me and set my body and mind at ease. Later, a bright, shiny, almost full moon transported me to a larger perspective. I met neighbors on my walk, and we laughed as we complained that daylight saving time had ended and we could barely see one another. Yet, even as shadowy figures, we were happy to run into one another. That night, I talked with a friend about the day's events. We laughed about the way my mind worked. She said hers also worked that way, and she could identify with me.

Before going to bed, I picked up some of my Buddhist books and read reminders that thoughts are just thoughts and underneath all those sometimes crazy, swirling, disturbing, floating, and ephemeral orbs, all is well.

And who knows, perhaps after another emotional day at the doctor's office or anywhere else my see-sawing mind begins to kick in, I can stop it before it starts or slow it down, and try to take it all in stride before I go on my next rollercoaster ride.

Sister Loss

I am a woman who lost her sister

but she has not left me for good.

She comes back from the land of the

dead when I need her, when I've had

too much of the world—I call her name.

She doesn't come all the time or right away.

She waits until I'm alone in the quiet of my

home looking at stars—wondering about

everything I don't understand and can't

control. That's when she comes and takes

my hand and walks with me, assuring me

of her love, letting me know she's heard me

and will accompany me through all the confusion.

I feel the questions I have about what's happening now—all the dying, people dying, the earth dying, democracy dying. All these things I must admit I can't control—I want to but I can't.

So what I need now is comfort from the sister I've loved for so long, trusted, connected with. The sister who followed me to the same college— me a senior about to graduate, she an incoming freshman who thought I was so cool—listened to me, laughed with me until we wet our pants.

The High Cost of Loving

WHY DOES IT HURT SO MUCH when we or our loved ones suffer? Who built suffering into the construct that made us anyway? My worry list grows longer and longer for the people I love: their deaths, injuries, and illnesses. A friend's father, when similarly worried, said it was the high cost of loving, but he wouldn't have it any other way because the cost of loving is well worth it.

All major religions hold a central place for suffering. It seems built into our lives. For Christians, the image of Christ languishing and dying on the cross is enough said about suffering. The toll that suffering takes on our bodies, minds, and hearts is so huge that I question it and wonder if we could ditch the suffering and just keep the joyful parts of life.

But it's always something, isn't it? You're vertical one moment, and the next, you've slipped on unseen water in the bathroom and you're down for the count. This happened to me once. In the Midwest, they immediately say, "It could have been worse" after such a mishap. So true. My doctor breathed a sigh of relief when only a broken toe showed up on the X-ray, and all I had to do was "buddy wrap" it to the adjoining good toe to let it heal. It could have been worse.

On the upside, it was relaxing to take a little staycation from obligations and activities and spend time nursing my toe back to health and happiness. That is, until an email arrived to let me know that my younger brother had an infection in his shoulder, which had been operated on several weeks before, after he lost his balance and slipped on the muddy part of a golf course. He was back in the hospital and would have to undergo another operation. "Atrocious," my older brother wrote in response to the news. I thought that nailed it for both of us.

I had just gotten used to the healing routine with my toe. Now I had to add another bead to the mental worry bracelet I carried in my psyche. And another soon followed when I learned that my sister, whom I thought was doing well, was experiencing severe anxiety again.

Then, yet another email came in about a distant cousin, Clayton, who was dying at the ripe old age of 103. He had survived Pearl Harbor, his son's suicide, and the stress of caring for his wife with Alzheimer's. His resilience and longevity balanced out some of my worry about other family members. I focused on connecting with two younger cousins to make sure they knew about Clayton's death.

A cousin who kept me abreast of celebrations and funerals had died several years before, so I was forced to resort to the internet to find the cousins I wanted to contact. I'd corresponded with them in the past and knew they were in their upper nineties. What I didn't know is that both of them were now deceased. I studied their online obituaries for any living progeny I could connect with, while taking in the disturbing reality that our family was shrinking! We had lost my younger sister the year before, so my most immediate family was already fewer in number. And the death of my eighteen-year-old dog, Ruby, a few months later opened up vast fields of loss in my current life.

Sadly, we were losing the older generation, and though they were not intimately part of my current life, I could not shake the visual image of a shrinking, disappearing family.

I'd been the family historian, or kinkeeper—a term I recently learned about to describe someone who keeps the family connections going—for long enough to know this was the natural order of things for any family. None of us knows our expiration date, and no amount of crying, counseling, or moving on with life can change the losses.

I'd learned after the death of my dear sister and my beloved fur friend to find solace in the beautiful birds outside the sliding glass door of my office. One bluebird came for a long period of time and seemed almost human in the way he hung out at the feeder and looked at me. My sister loved birds, and I thought of the bluebird as a sign she was communicating with me. Then he stopped coming, but a finch with red on his head and chest started to show up. His movements in the red planter next to the feeder reminded me of our dog bounding about. Life was back.

I was disturbed when the neighbors advised me to empty my bird feeder because of a salmonella outbreak among wild birds. I couldn't do it and kept waiting for the finch who had kept me company. He never came.

Now what, I thought? I could plant the nasturtium and poppy seeds I'd bought and take comfort knowing they would be germinating under the soil, showing me their bright colors at the exact right time, if I were patient.

Eventually, it was my encounter with Ben, the darling kid down the block, that brought me back to the present and gave me renewed trust in the ways of the world. He was riding in his car seat when his dad saw me walking and waved to me. The car was going too fast to see Ben, but soon after it passed, it circled back again. His dad said Ben was disappointed he didn't get to say hi to me. I looked at Ben as he stretched out his little hand. I held it and told him how thrilled I was that he wanted to say hi, how one of my favorite things was to see him, how I loved him. Ben giggled. The more positive things I said about my appreciation of him, the more he giggled.

I held onto his hand and realized that something would always circle back, as Ben and his dad had done. Something would always provide me with living proof that the high cost of loving was worth it, that the worry and sorrow for my loved ones would eventually find their place in the grand scheme of life.

Jason's Story

JASON CAME INTO MY LIFE THROUGH Tony. They both attended Antioch College, a liberal arts school in Yellow Springs, Ohio, in the sixties. Jason was a teacher's assistant in Tony's political science class. As an upperclassman, Tony looked up to the towering Jason, who was handsome, smart, and funny. When Tony failed one of his political science classes, Jason tried unsuccessfully to get the professor to excuse it, much to Tony's chagrin.

Although they didn't socialize much during the Antioch years, Jason gave Tony three pieces of sage advice: 1) let your hair grow, 2) lose weight, and 3) drop out of school. Tony never forgot Jason's counsel and eventually followed all three suggestions. He dropped out of Antioch in 1963. Several years later, he traveled to Afghanistan, where he lost weight and let his hair grow.

They were out of touch until 2000, when Tony saw Jason's name in *Common Ground*, Antioch's alumni magazine, which mentioned that he lived in Oakland, where we lived, so we invited him to dinner.

He arrived with a bouquet of flowers and a bottle of wine. We liked each other immediately, and the three of us enjoyed a lively, intelligent conversation, followed by many more as the years went on and our friendship grew.

We ate countless meals together in our home, and Jason had a lot of questions for Tony about the menu and preparation of these feasts. Tony was a graduate of the San Francisco Culinary

Academy, and Jason, who had only basic cooking skills, was always eager to try Tony's recipes on his own.

We watched the TV series *Big Love* and joked about how the movie club discussions became like therapy. Jason's psychological insights were sharp and helpful, even though he had a love-hate relationship with psychology. On the one hand, he could be sarcastic about concepts like letting go and trusting the universe; on the other hand, he waxed endlessly about psychological theories.

If we had a classical music station on when he visited, as we usually did, he often interrupted our conversation, "Oh, that's a Mahler piece. Let's listen." Or after listening to an aria from *The Marriage of Figaro,* he asked if we liked it. When we replied with a resounding yes, he said, "Lovely. What heavenly music. Let's all be happy."

One of the last gifts Jason bestowed upon me was to keep me company during a recent depression. He came over on Sundays for several months. He arrived at 11:00 a.m., and we sat in the backyard and talked about how we were both doing, with special emphasis on my depression. The sun was shining, the birds were chirping, and Jason was totally present with me. These "Sundays With Jason" were invaluable for my healing.

Before he died, Jason was in the hospital for several weeks. Frequently, he listened to Sibelius, humming and waving his arms to the music. Many friends came to visit and shared what he meant to them. One day, I visited him alone. He was days away from dying and hooked up to oxygen and large doses of morphine.

He looked at me and asked, "Any advice?"

"Let go?" I replied. We both smiled.

A small gathering held shortly after his death made it obvious that Jason had touched so many lives with his caring ways.

Ironically, many remarked, "He could have been a therapist!" I agreed and told my "Sundays With Jason" story.

At the gathering, I learned that Jason had visited his business partner, Randy, right up to the end of Randy's life. Randy had a transcription and editing business that he passed on to Jason. Randy's family and many friends did the same for Jason. He was insistent that visitors stay close where he could see and hear them. He wanted to be touched, listen to classical music, and converse while it was still possible. Eventually, he became too weak to talk, but one night he surprised those of us sitting by his bedside with his booming rendition of Edward R. Morrow's deep, rich voice. How he managed that, I'll never know.

After the memorial, Jason's good friend invited several of us to stop by Jason's apartment and take mementos. Tony picked up three wooden birds and a tile with a bird image on it. We didn't know Jason was so fond of birds. He was a mystery in many ways and had a sensitive side we didn't always see. We added the mementos to a memorial altar we created for him in our home. We took other things: a skillet, a knife, baskets, books, and a jacket—all items he had touched and used and which now serve to remind us of him.

Our world is not the same without Jason in it. There are no more talks about life and politics, or laughing over the smallest things. No more meals together. Where did he go? Did we take enough to remember him by? He was a good man, we often say. We miss him dearly.

THE FOLLOWING FOUR STORIES ORIGINALLY appeared in *Zichron, the Journal of the San Francisco Genealogy Society*. They are about Tony's relatives, who caught my interest and touched my heart.

Some of the material is woven into my 2018 book, *My Dear Good Rosi, Letters From Nazi-Occupied Holland 1940-1943*, regarding Tony's grandparents, who were murdered at Auschwitz in 1943.

Remembering Carla

CARLA KNOLLER WAS BEAUTIFUL, OUTGOING, CHARMING, and artistic, her cousin, Marion, told me. She and Carla, close in age, grew up and played together as children in Berlin. Marion was shy and in awe of Carla's vibrant personality and how easily she interacted with people. Everyone was drawn to her. Marion never showed jealousy when speaking of Carla, only love, appreciation, and admiration.

I'd seen family photos that confirmed Carla's beauty, but hearing Marion's memories of Carla made me eager to know more about her.

I began by speaking with the few relatives who had known Carla. All confirmed Marion's impressions of her, adding that Carla had been a skilled graphic artist. They pointed me to the US Holocaust Museum for further details about what had happened to Carla during the war. The museum led me to other valuable contacts and resources including the Institute for War, Holocaust and Genocide Studies (NIOD) in Amsterdam, and the Kamp Westerbork Memorial Museum, whose staff graciously helped me put together the pieces, not so much of Carla's life, but of her death.

Carla was seventeen, living in Amsterdam and attending art school when she received a summons from the German Nazi occupying power to present herself at Nazi headquarters for "work in the East." The Nazis had invaded the Netherlands in May 1940 and slowly began to impose restrictions on the

Jews; the same restrictions that had caused Carla and her family to flee from Germany to neutral Netherlands to escape Nazi persecution.

Despite the restrictions, the family gathered to celebrate the wedding of Carla's older sister, Ruth, in June of 1942 in Amsterdam. A month before, the Germans had issued a decree that all Jews over the age of six must wear the Jewish star on their outer clothing where it would be visible. There was no question of not complying. Ruth, her husband, the wedding party, and guests all wore the Star of David at the ceremony. Everyone smiled for the camera.

When the summons arrived the next month, Carla and her family were confused about the intent. They had never seen anything like it before and did not know how they should respond. They had not heard of Auschwitz or the plan to round up and deport all the Jews in Europe. They didn't know that seven months before, on January, 20, 1942, the most senior Nazi officials had met in secret in Wannsee, Germany, to formulate and complete plans for The Final Solution, the Nazi plan to eliminate Europe's Jewish population.

Carla's father, Ari, sought advice from the *Joodse Raad*, the Jewish Council, an organized group of Jews designated by the Germans to act as the liaison for communications between the Nazis and the Jewish community. Ari was told that Carla should report as the summons specified, or "something worse would likely happen."

On July 15, 1942, Carla and hundreds of other young Jews reported to the train station for the first transport of Jews from Amsterdam. They boarded the trains for Kamp Westerbork, a transit camp located several hours northeast of Amsterdam that had been built to house the many Jews who were escaping Nazi persecution in Germany.

The trains arrived at Westerbork, and the Jews were directed to a large hall filled with desks, typewriters, and personnel to register them. After registration, they were offered coffee and a roll and directed to other trains. Westerbork was not their final destination, and they boarded trains for Auschwitz-Birkenau.

Carla's family had no idea where Carla was taken. On September 29, 1942, three months after she'd left home, they received a postcard from her sent from Auschwitz-Birkenau. The arrival of the postcard is mentioned in documents from the Holocaust Museum, but not the content Carla had written. Historians who have researched mail sent during the war have documented that people in Carla's situation at Auschwitz were compelled to write something positive to their families to indicate they were alive and well.

Carla was murdered the next day, September 30, 1942. Her parents would not know for years she'd been murdered. After the war, they filed endless search documents with the Red Cross International Tracing Service for information about her whereabouts. In 1951, they were finally informed their daughter had been murdered during the war by the Nazis.

In letters written to family after the war, Ari expressed his deep regret that he had followed the advice of the Jewish Council to have Carla respond to the summons. He didn't know he would lose Carla forever. Once the family knew of Carla's murder, they submitted a Page of Testimony about Carla to add to the Hall of Names Memorial to Holocaust Victims at Yad Vashem in Jerusalem.

I add my own memorial to Carla with this story.

A Day in Eschau

WE TRAVELLED TO ESCHAU, GERMANY, TO see the town where Tony's great-great-grandfather, Peretz Loeb Mosbacher, and many Mosbacher ancestors had lived, and to visit the Jewish cemetery in Reistenhausen, five miles from Eschau.

We took an early morning train from Frankfurt to Aschaffenburg to connect with the Eisenfeld/Oldenberg train, where Otto Pheifer, the Eschau village historian, would be waiting for us. Our train from Frankfurt left four minutes late, and we missed our connection. The kindly station agent in Aschaffenburg called the Pheifer residence to tell them of the delay, and I frantically sent an email informing them that we would take the next train an hour later than planned.

This was our second glitch in getting to Eschau. We had planned to visit soon after our arrival in Germany, but because of problems with my passport, we were unable to visit until the end of our trip. I knew Germans were known for exactness and timeliness, yet neither one of our unforeseen changes seemed to matter to the people in Eschau. As we pulled into the station, I looked out the window and saw Otto standing on the landing with a big grin on his face. I knew right away that everything was fine and no apologies were needed for either delay. Posing for welcome photos was the first order of business, and then the drive in Otto's car to nearby Eschau.

I had done so much research on Eschau and the Mosbacher family that when I saw the sign announcing Eschau, I let out a little scream as if I didn't really believe there was such a place.

The day was packed with activities. First on the agenda was a visit to the restored town hall, where Otto's wife, Gertrud, awaited us, along with the former mayor, Ludwig Andreas Reidel, and his wife, the current mayor, Michael Gunther, and Dr. Jürgen Jung. It felt like old home week with all the smiles and handshaking, like we'd known one another long before this meeting. They offered us coffee and water, and directions to the restroom upstairs, before Dr. Jung invited us to sit in front-row seats and watch an informative video about the historical sites and landscape of Eschau.

Eschau has a population of only four thousand, a fact that thrilled me since I was born in a small town of seven thousand in rural Iowa. The village traces its roots back to 1285 when it was a thriving market town. It is located near the Main River in Lower Franconia, south of Frankfurt am Main, Aschaffenburg, and Würzburg, and surrounded by lovely green valleys and woodlands. There are castles that date back to the 1200s, which local residents are trying to preserve, restore, and boast about to tourists.

Otto had sent me photos of the house where the Mosbacher family had lived, including Tony's great-great-grandfather, who was born about 1785 and died sometime between 1856 and 1860. The photo caption read: "The solid half-timber construction of the house (formerly in the possession of the Feudal Lord of Eschau, the Count of Erbach), with its beautiful outer stairway, reveals the wealth of the owner, Berez Loew Mosbacher."

I was impressed with the photo and description of his beautiful home. I was glad that his work as a tradesman provided enough income to build several houses in the village, as well as to provide for his eight children: Chaim, Gudel Freund, Joseph, Fanny, Ricke, Emanuel, Sigmund (Tony's great-grandfather), and Adolph/Abraham.

The more I learned about Tony's great-great-grandfather, the more I liked him. According to town records, after the enrollment of Jewish families in the so-called Jewish Registers, he was the only one to use conventional first names instead of their Jewish first names, without seeking official permission to do so. The records state that Peretz "according to whim" signed himself Berez, Bernhard, or Lorenz.

This information and other facts were recorded in the manuscript of Eva Marie Schlicht, who researched and documented the early history of the Jews in Eschau. Her manuscript is in the possession of Otto Pfeifer. He uses it, along with others, to further document information about the Jews. Otto refers to himself as the "Eschau Mosbacher specialist."

When I asked why Eva and now Otto and his cohorts were interested in Jewish history, people seemed surprised by my question and responded that "these people lived in Eschau, were once our neighbors, and, of course, we want to know about them."

We took photos of the former home of Peretz and his family and had to admit, that even though the original structure was still standing, it was no longer impressive. The beautiful outer stairway depicted in the photo was gone, and the rest of the building had been converted to an electrical business.

We moved on and followed Otto to other spots he thought we'd be interested in, including the empty grass lot where the synagogue had once stood, the place where the *mikvah* (the place for a ritual Jewish bath) had been located. We saw the hooks in the old butcher shop where animals were ceremoniously slaughtered and hung. All these places were now something else or remained empty lots. It was hard to imagine that Jews had lived, worked, worshipped, and performed rituals in this village where no Jews had lived for seventy-seven years.

For this reason, the black plaque mounted on the outside of the old town hall with the names of Jews from Eschau who had been deported and murdered by the Nazis was a bit startling. We all lined up for a photo by the plaque, making sure it got the place of honor in the middle. The name, Lina Mosbacher, a descendant of Peretz's brother Feibel Mosbacher, was on the plaque. Lina was single. She had sold her home and left Eschau in 1934 to move into a Jewish retirement home in Frankfurt. From there, she was deported to Theresienstadt and murdered in Treblinka in 1942 at the age of seventy.

The one place that hadn't changed was the Jewish cemetery located five miles from Eschau in the town of Reistenhausen. Jews do not bury their dead in the same place they lived, so in the years before automobiles, Jews from Eschau walked or went by horse and buggy the five miles to bury their loved ones in Reistenhausen.

I knew Peretz was buried there after having received a photo of his tombstone from another relative, Joel, who had visited Eschau and the cemetery earlier in June. The gate to the cemetery was locked. Mr. Reidel, the former mayor, had the key and opened the gate for us. Once inside, we were back in time, scanning rows and rows of old tombstones streaked with green moss and inscribed with Hebrew words to honor the dead. No vandalism was evident. The only damage was from the roots of a large tree that had grown under one or two tombstones. The search for Peretz's tombstone was somewhat difficult because of the angle of the hill. We looked for large sticks to balance ourselves. Mr. Reidel, who stayed behind, offered me the use of his sturdy walking stick.

To help identify the tombstone of Peretz, Tony took the photo Joel had sent, and we all spread out to check headstones, periodically returning to Tony and the photo to confirm the shape and lettering of the stone we were looking for. I made a quick, silent plea to Peretz for help locating his monument. I felt comfortable in my firm reminder to everyone that we had not come all this way to fail.

Fairly soon, we heard Gertrud shout, "This is it. I've found it!" We all rushed to where Gertrud stood and compared the actual stone to the photo. This was definitely it, and the excitement of that moment grew as we gathered around the stone and placed rocks on it, a Jewish symbol of remembrance. Seeing Tony standing beside the tombstone of his great-great-grandfather, with all of us gathered around him, gave me goosebumps. We'd traveled far, seen the village where the Mosbacher ancestors had lived, and now stood where they were buried; the place that hadn't changed with time and that ironically felt most alive.

A friend, Saar, had translated the words inscribed in Hebrew on the tombstone after I had received the photo, so I knew the meaning of the words:

Here a precious jewel is buried

A head of the congregation of his community

He did acts of charity at all times

He endeavored to keep the commandments of the Pact

He sang with his voice at the house of God

He imbibed from the Mishna and Gemara

Peretz Ari son of Gershon (of Blessed Memory)

It wasn't clear if Peretz was a cantor or if he simply enjoyed singing in the synagogue. Either way, I added it to the growing list of things I liked about him.

There are no Jewish tombstones in the cemetery with dates after 1938. This small village experienced the same anti-semitism that Jews in large cities were subject to. The lucky ones found ways to get to the US or Palestine. The others were rounded up and murdered. Peretz died a natural death between the ages of seventy and seventy-five. His descendants were not so fortunate. His grandson, Hugo, and Hugo's wife, Clemy (Tony's grandparents), were murdered in 1943 in Auschwitz. Hugo was sixty-three, and Clemy was fifty-seven.

A Mosbacher family tree compiled in 1933 and updated in 1947 lists many family members who offered help to their relatives in Germany and saved them from the Nazis. Some family members were able to establish a new life in the United States. Unfortunately, not all on the family tree were saved. Having seen where Peretz, one of the elders of the Mosbacher family, lived and is buried, offers us some solace.

Natalie and Kokoschka

Left to right: my brother, Dave, middle is painting of Natalie Baczewski in Leopold Museum, Vienna, at a retrospective of Kokoschka's paintings. On the right is Dave's wife, my sister-in-law, Carolyn.

Courtesy of Dave and Carolyn Vasos

MY HUSBAND, TONY, AND I COULD never have predicted the surprises that awaited us on our trip to Vienna in June of 2018. The occasion? To attend a ceremony sponsored by the Stones of Memory Association to commemorate the laying of a stone of remembrance for Tony's paternal grandmother, Natalie Baczewski, who was murdered by the Nazis at Maly Trostenets, on September 18, 1942. In preparation for the ceremony, they asked us to send photos and any information we had about Natalie for a booklet the association was creating.

We didn't know much about her, and Tony had never met Natalie. Clearly, he was saddened and angered that his grandmother had been killed for the "crime" of being Jewish. So, we became interested in putting together a picture of what we supposed was Natalie's full, rich life as a mother, wife, and sister, from the few scraps of information we had. Elizabeth David Ben Hindleer, the founder of the association, encouraged our desire to focus on Natalie's life rather than her unjust and gruesome murder when she said, "Not to remember the murders but the life—the stones we set brings the victims back into our lives."

Tony recalled his father, Alexander, telling him how playful Natalie had been with him and his brother, Victor, when they were children, adopting the same height by sitting on her knees during playtime. She was funny, dramatic, and a great storyteller, using different voices for her characters.

Another relative mentioned that Natalie and her husband, Max, were well-to-do, lived in a comfortable, well-appointed apartment in Vienna, and had a summer home in Mölding outside the city. She said Natalie's sense of fairness and generosity were unparalleled, as described in the following story.

Natalie and Max were visiting his younger sister, Mathilda, who lived close to them. Natalie excused herself from the conversation taking place in the living room and went into Mathilda's kitchen. She had brought measuring tools with her and proceeded to take the measurements of her sister-in-law's kitchen flooring without anyone knowing about it. Several days later, workers from a flooring company came to Mathilda's house to install new flooring, which Natalie had paid for. It was a complete surprise to Mathilda. I can only imagine Natalie's delight at pulling this off.

According to Tony's father, Alexander, she and Max belonged to a progressive community, and Natalie was involved in abortion rights through various programs initiated by the ideas of Margaret Sanger.

Natalie's mother died when Natalie was two. Her four siblings were living on their own, and Natalie lived with her father, Sigmund Steinhaus, in Vienna. She became engaged to Max Baczewski, a successful patent attorney, in 1907. She wanted to give Max a painting of herself as a wedding present. Natalie and her father went to the School of Arts and Crafts at the Austrian Museum of Art to seek a talented painter to do the portrait. Oskar Kokoschka, a student at the school, was recommended. He later became one of Austria's greatest Expressionist painters. Kokoschka came to the Steinhaus home for many days as Natalie sat for her portrait. A niece of Natalie's who visited during this time remembered seeing Kokoschka painting the portrait and also enjoying lunch with the family.

Tony's father knew nothing of these details. He only knew that Kokoschka had painted a portrait of his mother and that his older brother, Victor, had acquired it after the war. It was hanging in Victor's home in Berlin until 1973. On his deathbed, Victor married his long-time companion, Birgit, and without telling his brother, left the painting to her. Of course, the painting meant a great deal to Alexander, and he resented Victor's decision.

Birgit kept it for several years and then sold it to a gallery. It went from gallery to gallery and to private collectors until 2015, when it was acquired and exhibited at a gallery in Pöchlarn, Austria, a few hours from the birthplace of Kokoschka and Vienna.

We found out about the painting from Eduard Wexberg, whom we met at Natalie's ceremony. Eduard and his wife, Anna, live in the same building at Waltergasse 4 where the Baczewskis lived. They invited us and the forty people in attendance to use the large, elegant lobby of the building for Natalie's ceremony. Everyone crowded in, listened while we spoke of Natalie, and showered us with support for honoring her.

We were thrilled to be in the same place where Natalie and her family had been, and we imagined them in the lobby as they went in and out of apartment sixteen on the second floor every day.

We hadn't mentioned the painting to Eduard, but he, like me, was a family historian and was researching what he could find online about the Baczewski family. When he found the image of Natalie's portrait hanging in the gallery in Pochlarn and sent it to us, we were astonished and immediately contacted the gallery to arrange a time to see the painting. The owner told us the painting was no longer at his gallery and had been given to the Leopold Museum in Vienna on permanent loan. Through others who had been at the ceremony, we made contact with the curator, Heike Elpeldauer, and the director, Hans-Peter Wipplinger, at the Leopold to see the painting.

The painting was in the museum's archives. We met a staff person in the lower level of the Leopold, and she rolled out a painting. She removed the protective cover and said, "Here it is." No! It wasn't Natalie. She looked carefully at the identification and exclaimed, "You're right, this is Mrs. Fisher." I was worried they had lost Natalie, but soon another painting was rolled in, and it was, to our great relief and awe, the portrait of Natalie.

Several staff members of the gallery had their iPhones ready, and the very first picture they wanted was of Tony standing next to the portrait of his grandmother. Tony obliged, and then the rest of us joined him next to the painting. When I forwarded the photo to Eduard, he noted that Tony and Natalie's hands were in the very same position. The rest of us had been too emotional and excited to notice. We later learned that Kokoschka placed special emphasis on the hands of the subjects he painted.

We had a million questions for Heike and the director about where the painting had been and how it was in the possession of the Leopold. The painting was one of Kokoschka's earliest works, and when the director saw it at the Pöchlarn gallery in 2015, he negotiated with the owner to let the Leopold Museum have it on permanent loan. A Kokoschka retrospective was scheduled in April 2019, less than a year away, and Natalie's portrait would be an important part of the exhibit. Because it was the earliest work in the collection, her portrait would be the first painting displayed in the retrospective,

Tony and I would not be able to attend, but I gave Heike a copy of the book created for Natalie's remembrance ceremony, which included information about her. Heike assured us they would put the text next to Natalie's painting for the retrospective. She also agreed to give us a provenance report that the Leopold would generate to document the history of the painting.

The elephant in the room was whether Tony and his brother, Steve, the grandchildren of Natalie and the only living descendants, had a claim to the painting. This question required further research, and it was ultimately decided that because no "Nazi pilfering" could be shown in the provenance report, Tony and his brother did not have a claim. For a time, we couldn't let go of the idea that, as direct heirs, they had a right to the painting. I'd seen a movie about a family reclaiming a painting, but couldn't recall the details. Later that night, I called my movie buff sister, Linda, from Vienna. She told me about the film, *A Woman in Gold*, which documented a family's success in establishing a rightful claim to Gustav Klimt's famous painting. We hoped for a similar outcome for Kokoschka's painting of Natalie, but it was not to be.

At our next family reunion, I related our experiences in Vienna and mentioned the upcoming Kokoschka retrospective where Natalie's portrait would be exhibited. Everyone showed an interest in the story. My younger brother, David, and his wife, Carolyn, would be in Switzerland during the time of the retrospective and entertained the idea of a side trip to Vienna to "visit Natalie."

I let the museum staff know of this possibility, and Dave and Carolyn connected with Heike's assistant, Aline. She told them to pick a day to visit the Leopold. They randomly chose Tuesday, not knowing this was a day the museum was closed. This was not a problem for Aline, who sent them a map with an arrow pointing to a private entrance they could use. They had the rare experience of being alone in the museum and having the personal attention of Aline to "introduce" them to Natalie, hear stories of Kokoschka, and ask any questions they had—an enlightening and unforgettable day by any measure.

Two other friends, Judy and Tom, happened to be in Vienna that summer and went to the Leopold to visit Natalie. Both couples took photographs next to her portrait and sent them to us. Natalie suddenly seemed so alive and popular! Just when we thought our happiness meter was full with the abundance of surprises regarding Natalie, a print of her portrait arrived from the Leopold, a gift from Dave and Carolyn. We had the print framed, and it hangs in a prominent spot in our home where Natalie can look at us and remind us that you never know what lies ahead.

Tony and I had ventured to Vienna for a ceremony to honor Natalie's death with a stone of remembrance, only to connect with a large group of people who magically expanded the experience and helped bring Natalie back to life. Eduard and Anna remind us periodically that they are watching Natalie's stone in front of Waltergasse 4. When recent construction was done on the building, they were careful to cover the stone to avoid any damage to it.

We did not get possession of the Kokoschka painting of Natalie. But as the founder of the "Stones of Memory" believed, Natalie has been brought back into our lives by so many who connected with her in Vienna during and after our journey there in 2018, a trip we will never forget.

Unclaimed

Ruth Knoller & Philip de Paauw on their wedding day
in Nazi occupied Amsterdam, June 16, 1942.

Courtesy of the Forum Verlag, Leipzig

THIS PHOTO OF THE WEDDING OF Ruth and Philip de Paauw appears in two books published in the early 1990s: *Between Dignity and Despair: Jewish Life in Nazi Germany* by Marion Kaplan and *Star of David and Christmas Tree: Memories of Survivors of Leipzig* compiled by Bernd-Lutz Lange.

The photo was sent to Ruth's aunt, Lea Nathansen, and her husband, Gabriel, in Leipzig, Germany, and hidden in a sealed box by a non-Jewish neighbor during the war.

I had corresponded with Ruth for many years. She lived in Bat Yam, Israel, and was as kind, open-hearted, and as down-to-earth as my mother-in-law, Rosi, had described her. Rosi shared stories of the family's time in Amsterdam, including their arrest and deportation first to Westerbork Transit Camp, and from there to Bergen Belsen concentration camp in 1944.

Fortunately, they were not sent to Auschwitz, the usual destination from Westerbork, where her younger sister, seventeen-year-old Karla, and other family members were sent and murdered. Ruth and her family had obtained passports for Ecuador, which made them eligible for a possible prisoner exchange at Bergen-Belsen. They received the passports but did not use them for such purposes. However, securing them may have protected them from extermination.

By the time of their arrest, Ruth had given birth to her first son, Ronny (Aron). He was six weeks old when she placed him with a non-Jewish, unmarried woman who lived a short distance from Amsterdam. Ruth wrote in a letter that "she saved his life while we were gone." Not all Jewish families who placed their children in hiding were able to reclaim them after the war, but Ruth was lucky not only to retrieve her son but also to remain in contact for many years with the woman who had cared for him.

Ruth had endured a great deal, but her spirit stayed strong, and, at least in our letters, she expressed no bitterness over the circumstances of her life. The gentle smile evident in her wedding photo seemed to have stayed with her throughout her life. She had never mentioned Lea or any of the Nathansens in her letters, but they turned out to be pivotal in the discovery of Ruth's wedding photo.

By complete chance, Ruth had seen Marion Kaplan's book in a bookstore in Israel. She told a professor who knew Marion that she was the bride in the photo. The professor told Marion the identity of the bride and the story of how Ruth had sent the photo to her Aunt Lea Nathansen in Leipzig. The Nathansens, in turn, took the photo and other items they wanted saved during the war to their non-Jewish neighbor, Hans Zaspel, a plumber. They delivered these items in a candy box, and Mr. Zaspel put the box in a zinc container and welded it shut for safekeeping.

The photo remained hidden in the sealed box for almost fifty years until Bernd-Lutz Lange went to Leipzig and made contact with the Jewish Religious Community of Leipzig to help him research information about the survivors of the Holocaust, including the Nathansens. He met the son of Hans Zaspel, who had almost forgotten about the box his father had hidden for the Nathansens. He retrieved it from its hiding place and showed Mr. Lange the contents, which included the photograph of Ruth's wedding, two *mezuzot* (small parchment scrolls), and private documents. He said the Nathansens had expressed their intention to reclaim the possessions after the war. It seems unlikely, but the Nathansens may have held out some hope at the time. They had signed a contract known as a *Heimeinkaufsverträg* (Home Purchase Agreement), disguised as a contract for lifelong community accommodation in a retirement settlement for Jews where housing, medical care, food, and washing were provided in exchange for signing over all their assets and possessions to the Nazis. The true destination, Theresienstadt Ghetto, is never mentioned in the document. It was a complete scam perpetrated by the Nazis to obtain the assets of Jews while providing a non-existent retirement home.

The Nathansens never returned to claim the box of possessions from Mr. Zaspel.

They were sent to the Theresienstadt Ghetto on September 20, 1942. Gabriel became ill due to the overcrowded, unsanitary conditions in the ghetto and died there on May 3, 1944. Lea was sent to Auschwitz on October 9, 1944, and was murdered upon arrival.

For a time, all that remained of the Nathansens was held in the box Mr. Zaspel had hidden. Despite never being able to reclaim what they left behind, they are still known and remembered in many ways.

The box is in the possession of the Jewish Community; the contents were sent to Gabriel's relatives in Israel, and the *mezuzot* are being used by his family there. In 1999, Ruth submitted Testimony to Yad Vashem for her Aunt Lea. Family in Israel submitted testimony for Gabriel.

Marion Kaplan's book with the photo of Ruth's wedding day, and her encouragement to pursue the mystery of how the photo was found, inspired the historical detective in me to follow all the clues and bring the Nathansens' story and their connection to Ruth into the light.

Acknowledgments

MANY THANKS TO MY FAMILY, FRIENDS, neighbors, and ancestors who have been with me on this journey from the heartland to California. Your continued encouragement and support is greatly appreciated.

My Friday morning writing group keeps my heart open and my fingers moving across the page. You are a very special group of women.

To Sandra Marinella, teacher and author of *The Story You Need to Tell*. Without her classes and my interaction with her, my stories may have remained hidden in file drawers and never seen the light of day.

Huge thanks to Gail Kearns of To Press & Beyond for skillfully coordinating all aspects of the creation of this book. This is the second time I've worked with Gail, and I hope there will be many more opportunities in the future.

To Peri Gabriel of Peri Gabriel Design for joining our team and bringing her visionary and creative design skills to bear on the cover and interior design.

Our family lost our youngest sister, Linda, in 2020. She was an avid reader who loved F. Scott Fitzgerald and Ernest Hemingway. In her unique loving style, she always supported me in my writing. Before she died, she urged all of us to "keep it going." May this book keep love and stories going long into the future.

And to my husband, Tony, for always being there.

Courtesy of City of Carroll, Iowa.

About the Author

JUDY A. VASOS is a historical detective who lives in Oakland, California, with her husband, Tony Baczewski. Judy's years of experience with social work, freelance writing, and the creation of unique family history books led to a deep appreciation and love of stories. Her experience growing up in Iowa surrounded by a large extended family of aunts, uncles, cousins, and grandparents, and her eventual move to California, along with the challenges of recreating herself there, led to a rich supply of material to write and tell stories.

Other books by Judy Vasos:

My Dear Good Rosi
Letters from Nazi-Occupied Holland 1940 - 1943

www.ingramcontent.com/pod-product-compliance
Lightning Source LLC
Chambersburg PA
CBHW060452080526
44584CB00015B/1416